D0468081

THE BIG BOOK OF AMERICA

Written by Roger Hicks
Illustrated by Sallie Reason, Helen Ward
Stella Stilwell *and* Dean Entwistle

TEMPLAR

A Templar Book

This edition produced for Reading's Fun Ltd,
119 South Main Street, PO Box 2370, 307 West Burlington,
Fairfield, Iowa 52556.

This book was designed and produced by
The Templar Company plc, Pippbrook Mill, London Road,
Dorking, Surrey RH4 1JE, Great Britain

Designer Janie Louise Hunt
Project Editor Wendy Madgwick
Proof reader and **indexer** Phebe Kinneston

ISBN 1–898784–23–X

Printed in Italy by L.E.G.O. S.p.A.

Contents

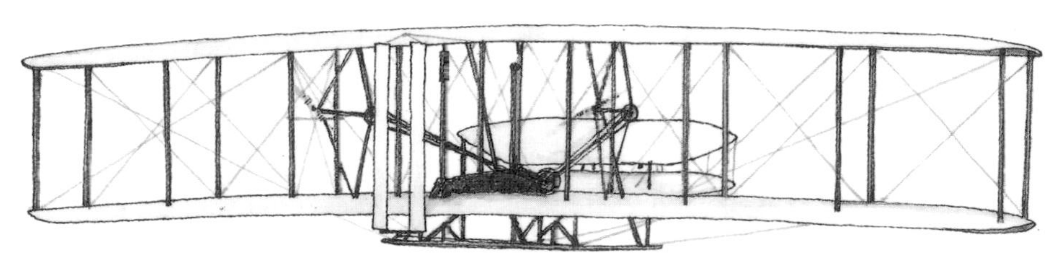

United States

of America

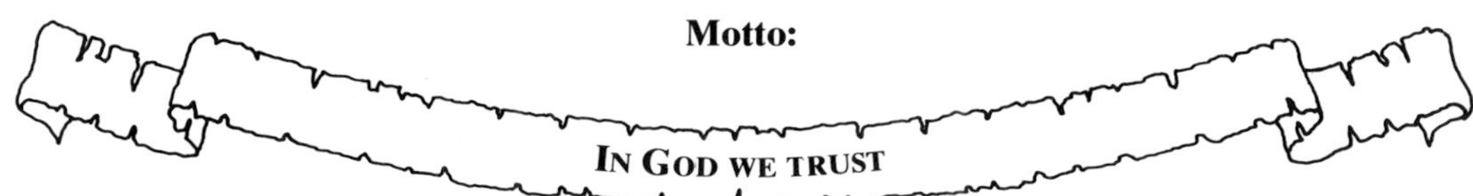

The United States of America is the richest country the world has ever seen, and for most of the 20th century it has also been the most powerful. Nor is it rich only in material wealth: it is rich in scenic wonders, and in the resources and variety of its people. Its history, although short by the standards of many nations, is also richer and more complicated than many people realize. The enormous diversity of the United States is obvious if one looks at the 50 states that make up the country, and its history can be charted by reviewing the order in which the states joined the Union.

The earliest explorers and settlers in what eventually became the United States were chiefly the Spanish, French, and British although Dutch, Russian and Swedish explorers were also prominent. The original British colonies in the east became very successful, but during the 18th century, conflict grew between the colonists and the British governors. The 13 colonies won

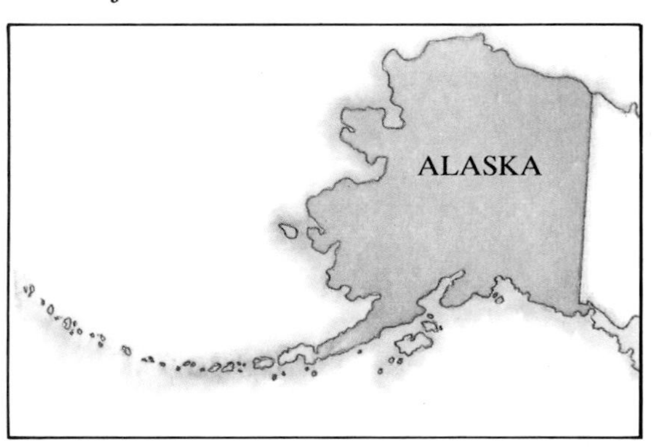

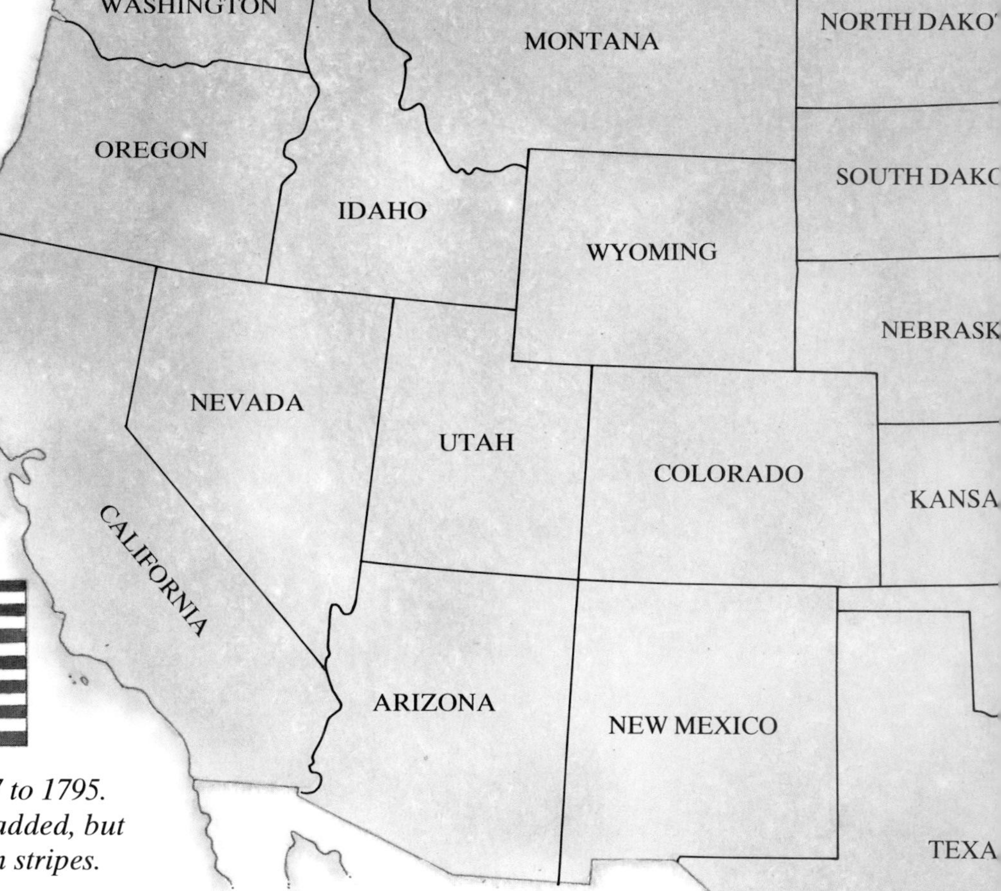

▶ Old Glory:
The "Stars and Stripes" carries a stripe for each of the original 13 colonies, and a star for each of the states. The original flag, with 13 stars "representing a new constellation" was used from 1777 to 1795. In 1795, two new stripes as well as two new stars were added, but since 1818 the flag has carried only the original thirteen stripes.

◀ Who "discovered" America?
The "American Indians" or Native Americans probably crossed the Bering Straits "land bridge" from Russia, up to 25,000 years ago. In about AD 1000, Leif Ericsson almost certainly reached what is now Nova Scotia. Columbus reached the West Indies in 1492, but never saw the continental land mass. It was not until the 1500s that European explorers "discovered" much of America.

independence in the Revolutionary War (1775–83). Expansion into the west of the country continued throughout the 19th century, and California was acquired after the Mexican War (1846–48). By 1820 the cotton-growing southern states were in conflict with the northern states, especially over slavery. This led to the Civil War (1861–65), which ended in victory for the North and the abolition of slavery. Industrial, economic, and territorial expansion followed with the purchase of Alaska and the annexation of Hawaii.

If this book has a historical bias, it is because a nation's past is the key to its present: as John F. Kennedy said, "Those who do not study history are condemned to repeat it." The guiding light in American history is, and always has been, an ideal of progress and freedom and equality which was responsible for the foundation of the country and which has burned fairly steadily ever since.

There have been times when that light has flickered; but always, there have been people who have upheld America's ideals and who have ensured that the light was never extinguished, people who could say, with the Reverend Martin Luther King, Jr., "I have a dream..."

Statue of Liberty
The Statue of Liberty Enlightening the World, a gift from the people of France to the people of the United States of America, has stood in New York Harbor since 1886. The copper-clad statue is just over 151 feet high from base to torch and weighs 225 tons. The island on which it stands was called Bedloe's Island until 1956, when the name was changed to Liberty Island.

Washington DC

The nation's capital, Washington, is not in any state. The District of Columbia was originally formed from land given by Maryland and Virginia. The idea was to make sure that no one state should claim or acquire special privileges merely because it was the home of the capital. The ten-mile-square site, chosen by George Washington, was established in 1791. The Virginian portion was given back to Virginia in 1846, so DC, as it is commonly known, is no longer a perfect square and is effectively bounded by Maryland.

Capitol Hill
The Capitol was named after the Capitoline Hill in ancient Rome, where the government met. It was designed by a self-taught architect, William Thornton, in 1793.

1

Delaware

The First State

On December 7 1787, Delaware ratified the new Constitution. The United States, which previously existed only on paper (after the Declaration of Independence), effectively came into being on that day.

The area was first explored by Henry Hudson in 1609. Although the Dutch built a settlement in 1631, the first permanent colony was founded by the Swedes in 1638. Delaware was later recaptured by the Dutch (1655) and then taken by the British (1664).

At first Delaware was part of Pennsylvania. It did not become a separate territory until 1704.

Delaware, the second smallest state after Rhode Island, is highly industrialized. Many large chemical companies are centered around Wilmington, which has been nicknamed "the chemical capital of the world." Motor vehicles, synthetic rubber, textiles, and food products are also made. Delaware's farmers produce chickens, soybeans, dairy products, and corn.

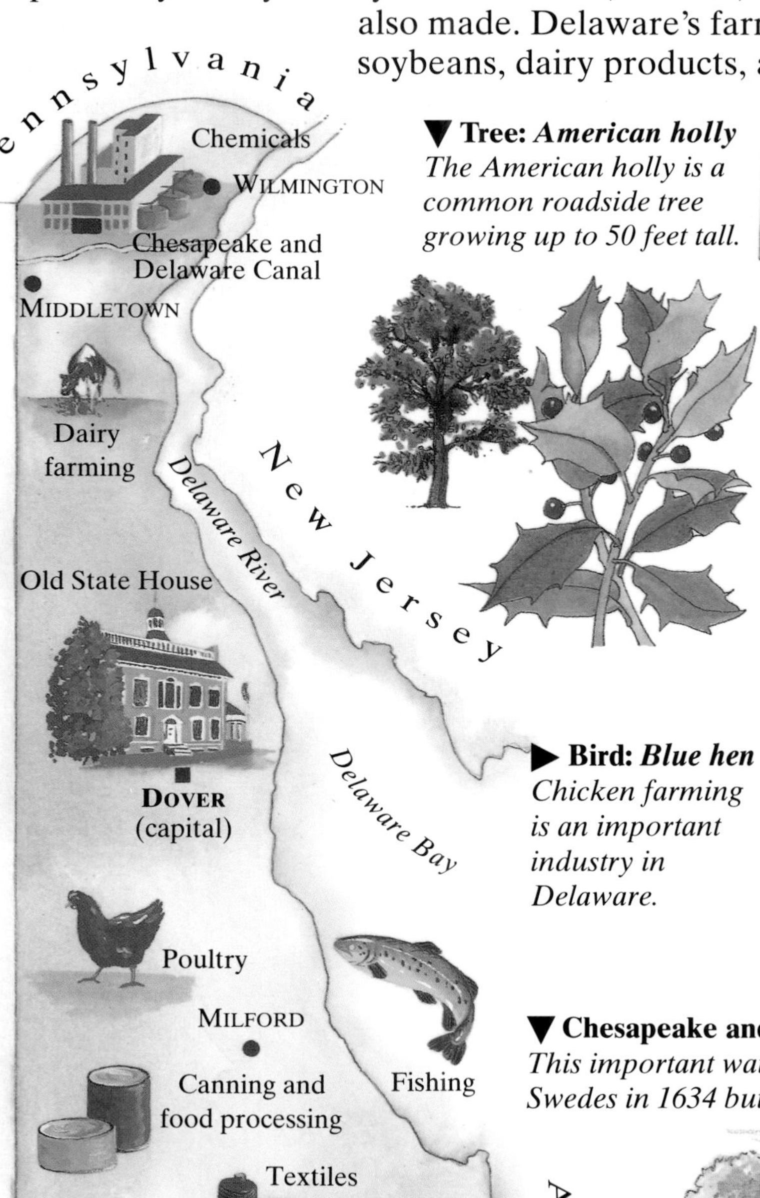

▼ State flag:
The state coat of arms on a buff lozenge against a blue background bears the proud date when Delaware became the first state.

▲ Flower: *Peach blossom*
Delaware, Maryland, and New Jersey were the first states to grow peaches commercially.

▼ Tree: *American holly*
The American holly is a common roadside tree growing up to 50 feet tall.

▲ Insect: *Ladybug*
These appealing insects are of great benefit to people as they feed on a variety of plant pests.

▶ Bird: *Blue hen*
Chicken farming is an important industry in Delaware.

▼ Chesapeake and Delaware canal
This important waterway was planned by the Swedes in 1634 but was not finished until 1829.

Pennsylvania

The Keystone State

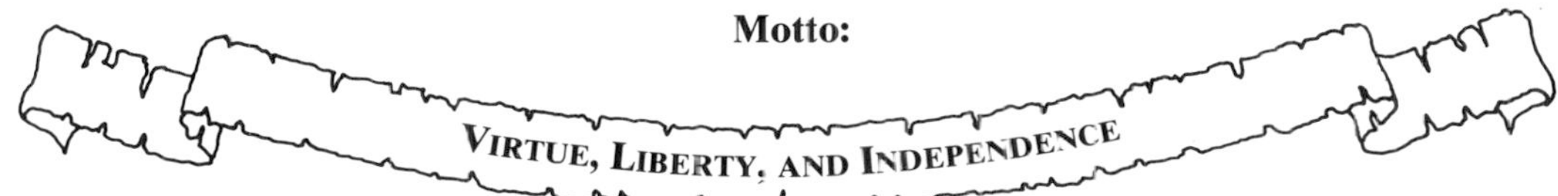

Pennsylvania was the 2nd state to join the Union, on December 12 1787. The Dutch, the Swedes, and the English all at one time claimed what later became the "Quaker State." By 1680 English control was well established and William Penn founded his state for the Society of Friends (Quakers). Penn guaranteed complete religious freedom for everyone. He treated the Native Americans fairly and they responded with friendship. Later, German and Scots–Irish settlers colonized the west, and the French claimed part of the interior. The local tribes were unhappy at this expansion and a time of unrest followed with the French and Indian Wars (1754–63).

Today, Pennsylvania is a major farming and manufacturing state making food products, machinery, chemicals, and cars and trucks. Oil refining is also important. Pennsylvania is a leading steel and iron producer, and much of America's hard coal is mined here.

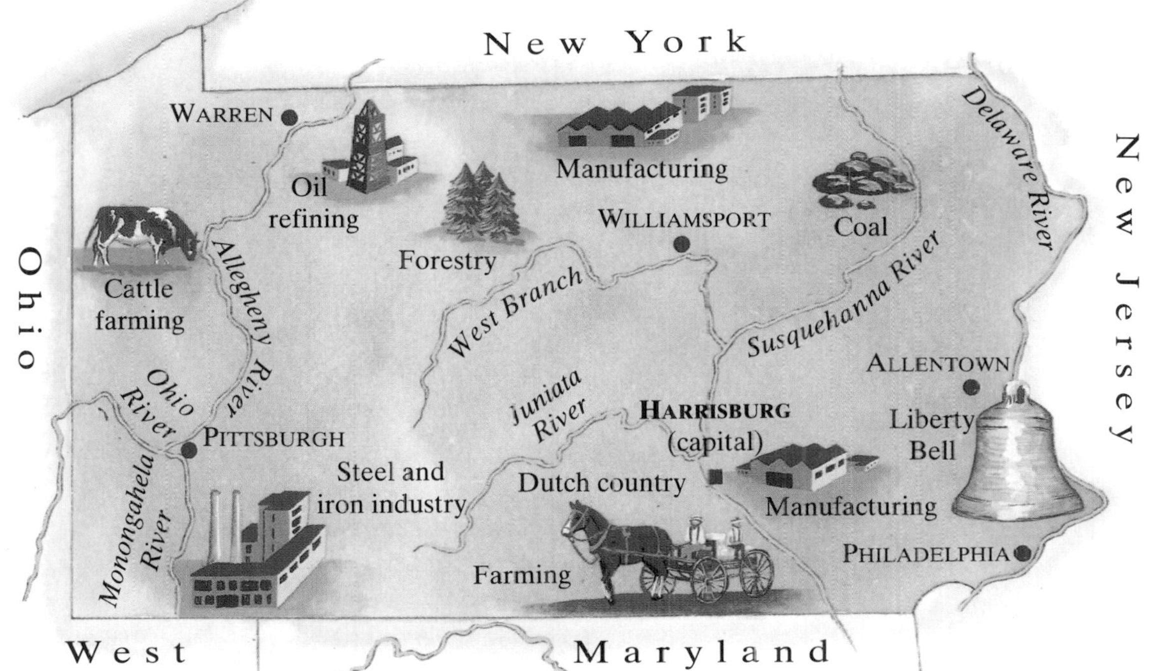

▲ **Flower:** ***Mountain laurel***
This evergreen shrub with its pink or white flowers is also called the calico tree or calico bush.

▼ **Tree:** ***Eastern hemlock***
Hemlocks, close relatives of spruce trees, can grow to 200 feet high.

◀ **State flag:**
The state coat of arms shows a sailing ship, a plow, and three wheatsheaves.

▶ **William Penn**
William Penn, an English Quaker, founded Pennsylvania. He drew up a constitution, "The Frame of Government," allowing freedom of worship and other civil liberties.

▲ **Bird:** ***Ruffed grouse***
This secretive bird of forest edges is called a partridge in the north and a pheasant in the south.

3

New Jersey

The Garden State

Motto:

New Jersey was the 3rd state to join the Union, on December 18 1787. The region was first explored in 1524. The earliest settlers were the Dutch in 1623, followed by the Swedes in 1638. The British then colonized the area until they were expelled by Washington and his army. The settlers seem to have co-existed well with the local tribes. When the last Native American claims were settled in 1832, their chief said, "Not a drop of our blood have you spilled in battle; not an acre of our land have you taken without our consent."

On the coastal plain, between the relatively low mountains, New Jersey has rich soils suitable for farming. A variety of crops are grown including vegetables and fruit. The farm products are exported to New York, just across the river, hence the name "The Garden State." One of the most urbanized and densely populated states, New Jersey is also a major industrial center. Its beaches and beautiful countryside attract many tourists.

▼ **State flag:**
The color of New Jersey's flag is said to be that chosen by George Washington for New Jersey troops during the Revolution.

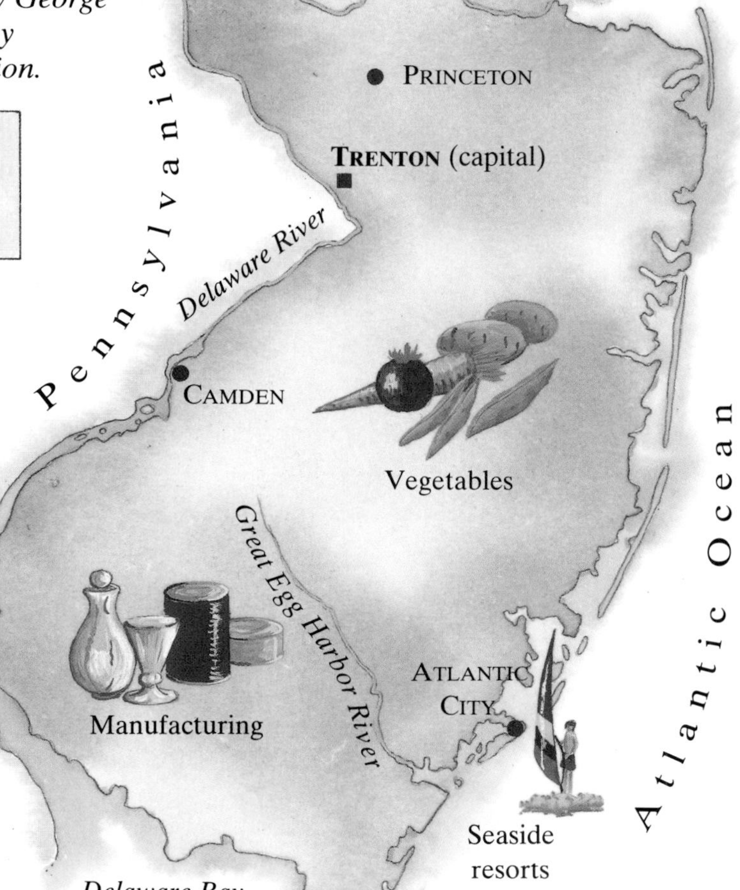

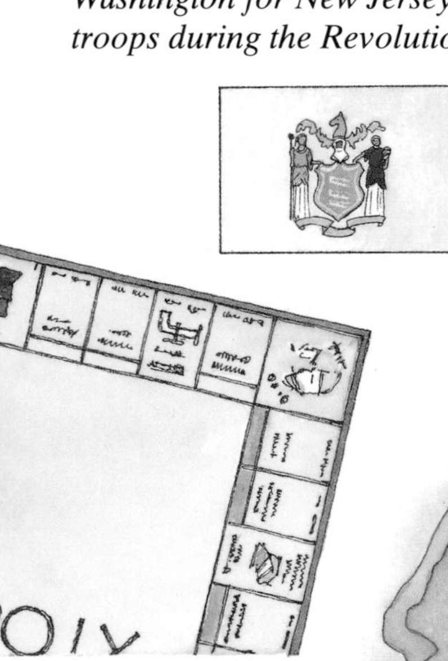

▲
Monopoly
The board game "Monopoly" is based on the streets of Atlantic City.

▼ **Tree: *Red oak***
The acorns of the red oak are hairy inside the nutshell, unlike those from the black or white oak.

▼ **Spring visitors**
Each spring, millions of migrating shorebirds such as sandpipers, turnstones, and plovers, stop on the Atlantic shores of New Jersey and Delaware. They feed on the eggs of millions of breeding horseshoe crabs.

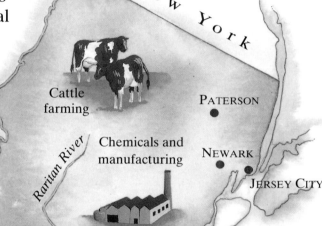

4

Georgia

The Peace State

Motto:

WISDOM, JUSTICE, AND MODERATION

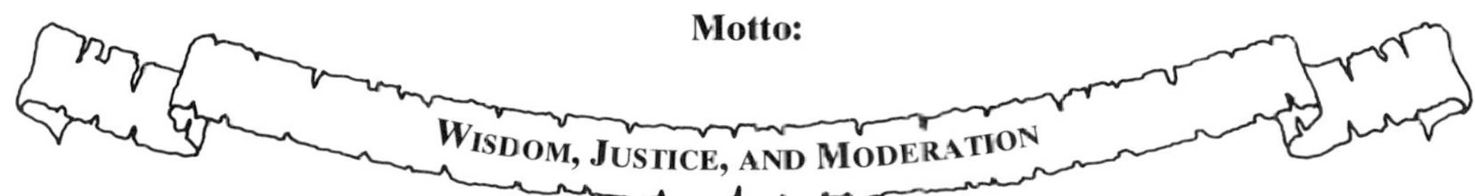

Georgia, named for King George II, was the 4th state to join the Union, on January 2 1788. First explored by the Spanish in 1540, Georgia was the last of the British colonies to be founded, in 1732. Early immigrants were English, Scottish, German, Piedmontese, Swiss, Portuguese, and Jewish. At first, Georgia was not involved in the Revolution, but it soon joined the Continental cause. After this, many more people moved to the region. During the Civil War, Georgia sided with the Confederacy. General Sherman's destruction of Atlanta (1864) and his "March to the Sea" did lasting damage, which was still evident well into the 20th century.

Today, Georgia is a fast-growing agricultural and manufacturing state. Traditional crops like tobacco and cotton are still grown, but fruit, peanuts, and livestock are of increasing importance. The main industries include textiles, transport chemicals, and processed foods.

▼ **State flag:**
The Confederate Battle Flag is combined with the state seal.

▼ **"King Cotton"**
"King Cotton" was the mainstay of the economy before the Civil War. It remains an important cash crop in some areas.

▼ **Flower: *Cherokee rose***
This trailing rose with its large white flowers was originally from China. It now grows in many parts of the United States.

▼ **Pre-war houses: *Ante-Bellum***
These pre-Civil War houses are a common sight in Georgia. They are a reminder of the way people lived, as well as of slavery. The adoption of Georgia on My Mind as the state song showed the increasing importance of black culture.

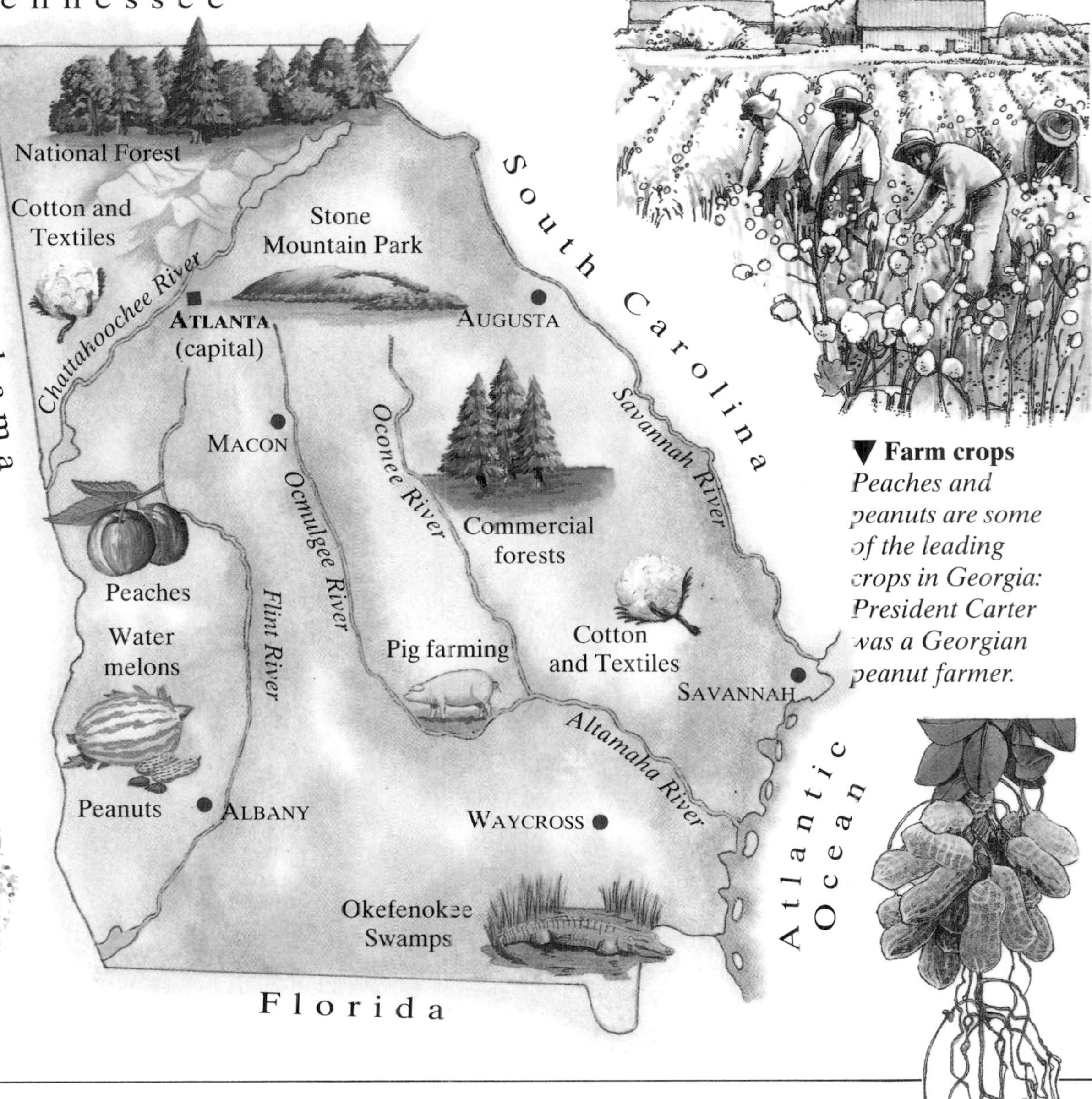

▼ **Farm crops**
Peaches and peanuts are some of the leading crops in Georgia: President Carter was a Georgian peanut farmer.

Map labels: Tennessee, National Forest, Cotton and Textiles, Stone Mountain Park, South Carolina, Alabama, Chattahoochee River, ATLANTA (capital), AUGUSTA, MACON, Oconee River, Ocmulgee River, Savannah River, Commercial forests, Flint River, Peaches, Water melons, Pig farming, Cotton and Textiles, SAVANNAH, Peanuts, ALBANY, WAYCROSS, Altamaha River, Atlantic Ocean, Okefenokee Swamps, Florida

5

Connecticut

The Constitution State

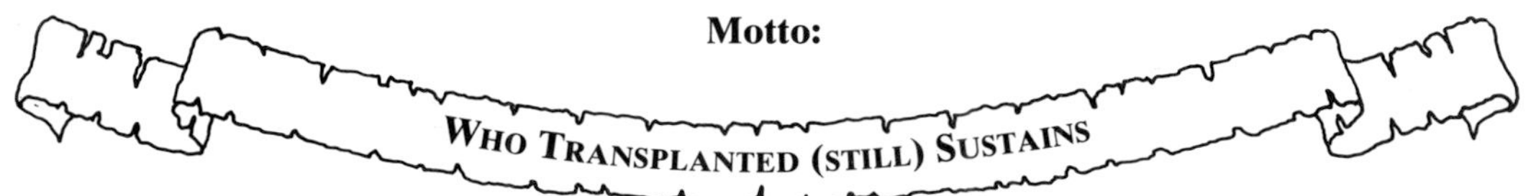

Connecticut, one of the original Thirteen States, was the 5th to join the Union, on January 9 1788. The area was first explored by the Dutch in 1614. British exploration followed and English colonists settled in the area from 1630 to 1660. During the Revolution, the state provided so much money and goods for the Continental Army that George Washington called it the "Provision State."

After the Revolution, the "Connecticut Yankee" became a byword for American inventiveness. Famous inventors include Eli Whitney, who made the cotton gin, Linus Yale of lock fame, and Charles Goodyear whose name still appears on automobile tires.

Yale University, the fourth oldest in the country, was founded in 1701.

The third smallest state, Connecticut is densely populated. Its many industries include helicopter and nuclear submarine construction and silverware. Some of the biggest insurance companies in the United States are based in Hartford.

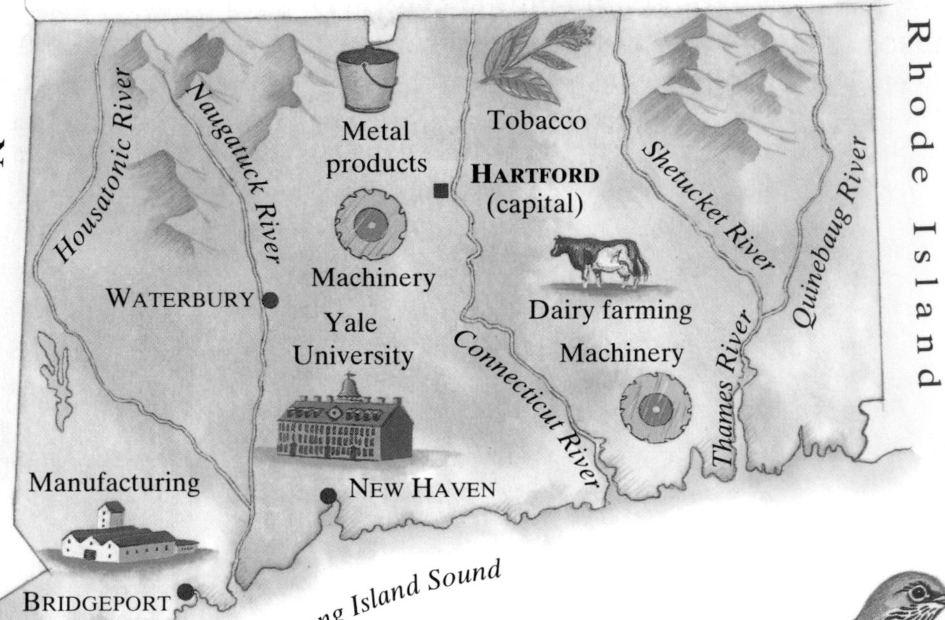

▶ **State flag:**
The three vines on the state coat of arms represent the three colonies which became the State of Connecticut.

◀ **Church and State**
In the early years, there was no separation of Church and State. There was even a "religious test" for citizenship.

▶ **Bird:** ***American robin***
The American robin is easily recognized. The chick has a spotted breast which soon turns a distinctive brick-orange.

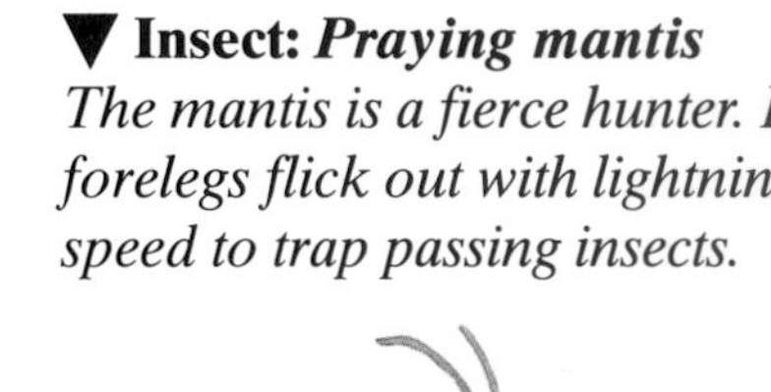

▼ **Insect:** ***Praying mantis***
The mantis is a fierce hunter. Its forelegs flick out with lightning speed to trap passing insects.

▲ **Animal:** ***Sperm whale***
Once, whaling was a major industry in the New England states. Now, the whale is a symbol of conservation.

▶ **Hero:** ***Nathan Hale***
Nathan Hale was hanged as a spy by the British in 1776. He was disguised as a Dutch schoolmaster and was only 21 years old.

Nathan Hale's Schoolhouse

6

Massachusetts

The Old Colony State

Motto:

BY THE SWORD WE SEEK PEACE, BUT PEACE ONLY UNDER LIBERTY

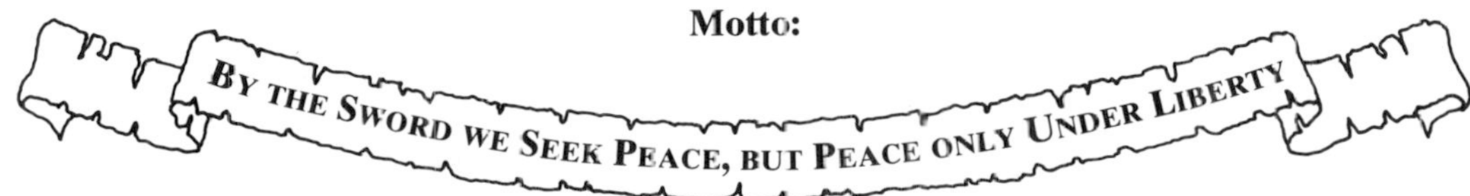

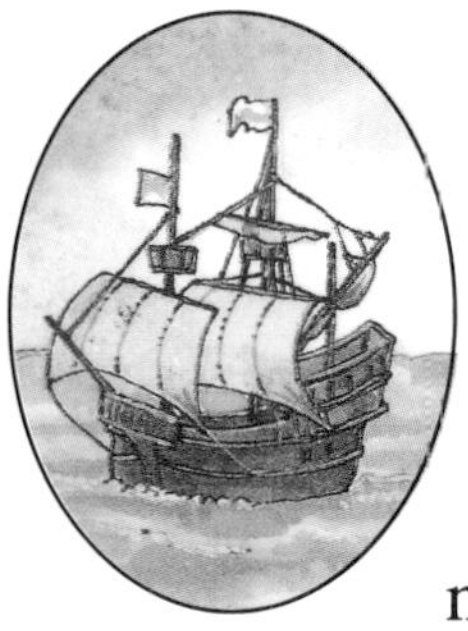

Massachusetts joined the Union as the 6th state, on February 6 1788. Its name comes from the Algonquian, and means "Near the Great Hill." The state has a long history. Norsemen may have landed near Cape Cod in 1003 and many Europeans visited the area in the 1500s. In 1614, John Smith explored and mapped the coast. The Pilgrim Fathers landed here in the *Mayflower* and founded the colony of Plymouth, Massachusetts around Christmas 1620.

The Revolution began in Massachusetts with the Boston Tea Party. Other colonies joined the uprising and the battles of Lexington, Concord, and Bunker Hill followed.

The invention of the power loom in 1814 boosted manufacturing in Massachusetts. The state rapidly became an industrial center and has remained so ever since. Today communications and electrical equipment, textiles, and metal and food products are the main industries. Farming centers on dairy produce, cranberries, and poultry. The state's many famous universities, including Harvard, have made Massachusetts an important center in the educational and cultural life of America.

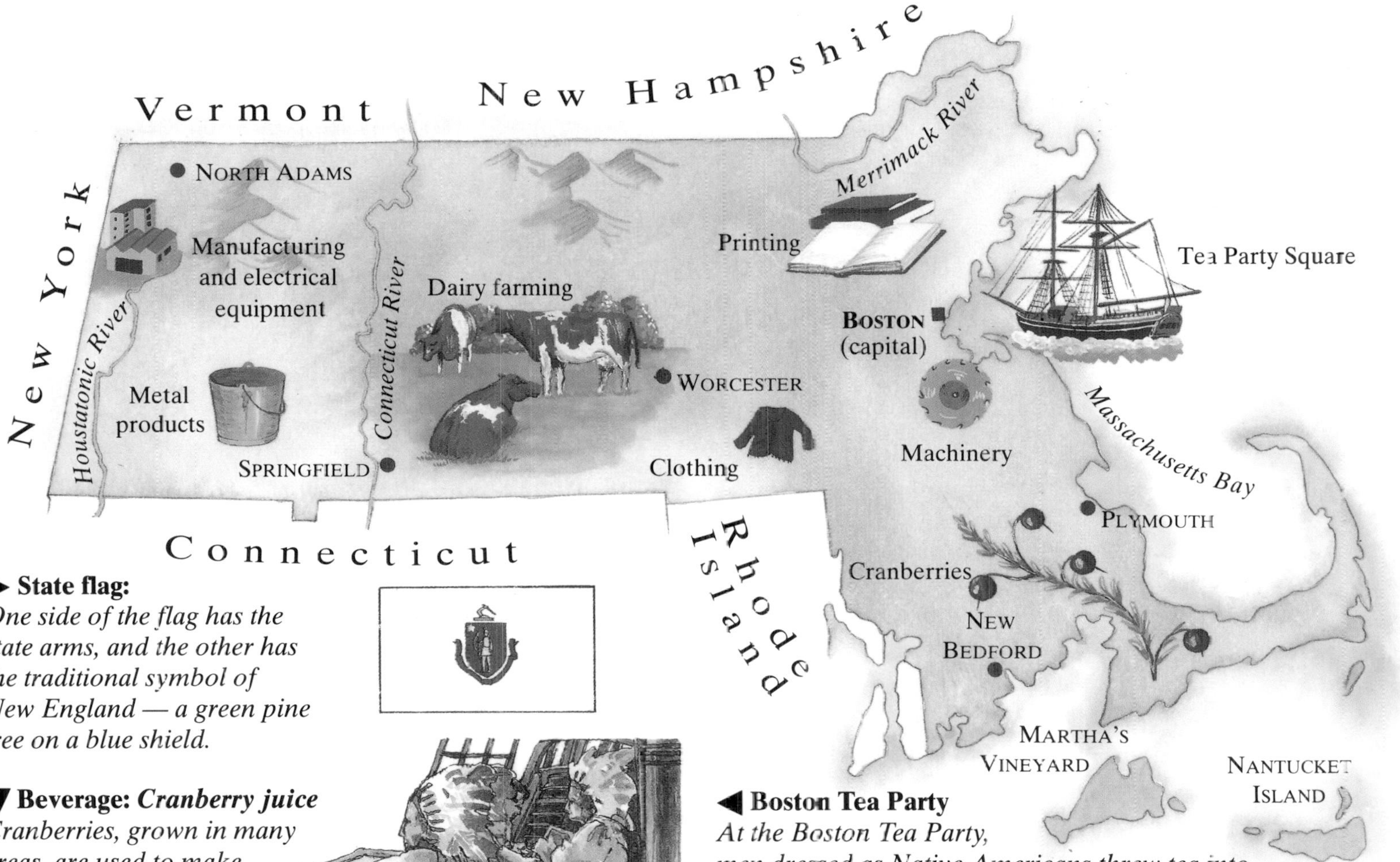

▶ **State flag:**
One side of the flag has the state arms, and the other has the traditional symbol of New England — a green pine tree on a blue shield.

▼ **Beverage: *Cranberry juice***
Cranberries, grown in many areas, are used to make cranberry juice and cranberry sauce.

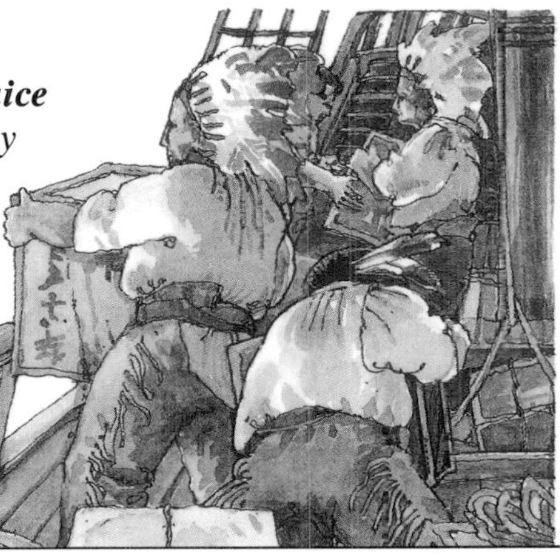

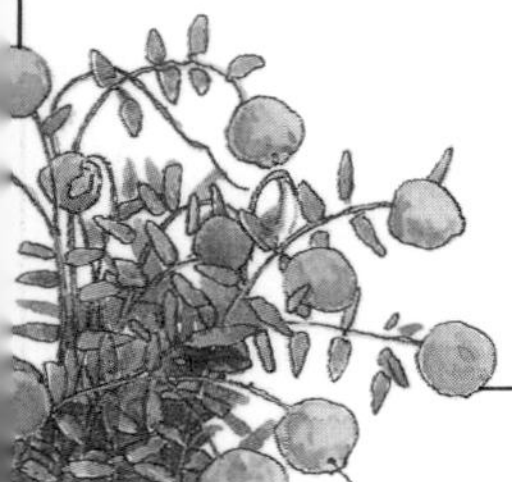

◀ **Boston Tea Party**
At the Boston Tea Party, men dressed as Native Americans threw tea into the harbor as a protest against English tea taxes.

▶ **Tree: *American elm***
This handsome tree, which can reach 120 feet in height, is prized for both its appearance and its timber.

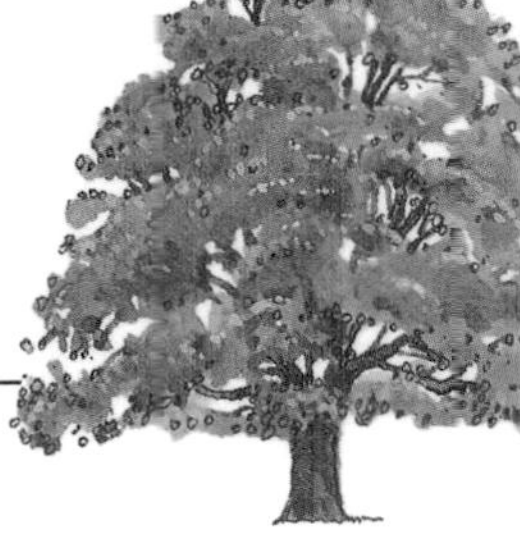

7

Maryland

The Free State

Motto:

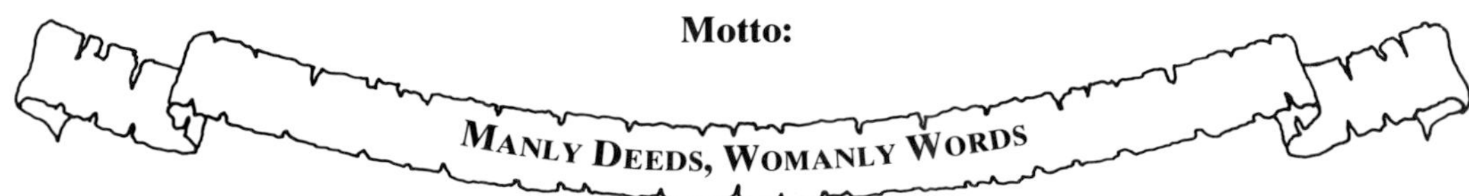

Maryland, named for Queen Henrietta Maria, wife of Charles I, joined the Union as the 7th state, on April 28 1788. The area was first explored in 1608 by Captain John Smith. The British colonized the region in 1634, building a settlement at St. Mary's City. Maryland took an active part in the Revolution, from the siege of Boston to the surrender of the British at Yorktown.

Today Maryland is a prosperous state, with thriving industries, farming, and fishing of many kinds. Chesapeake Bay oysters are famous countrywide. Shipping is also important. Baltimore is one of the nation's busiest ports and Annapolis is home to the United States Naval Academy. Maryland also provides services for the District of Columbia and the nation's capital, Washington.

The landscape is very varied. The Atlantic coast is mostly flat, rising to the piedmont plateau and then the Appalachian Mountains.

▼ **State flag:**
The arms of Lord Baltimore (yellow and black) are quartered with the arms of his mother's family, the Crosslands.

◀ **Bird: *Baltimore oriole***
This black and yellow songbird builds a distinctive hanging nest.

▶ **Flower: *Black-eyed Susan***
Also called the yellow daisy, this golden flower has a distinctive black center.

▶ **Francis Scott Key**
The unsuccessful British bombardment of Fort McHenry in 1812 inspired Francis Scott Key to write "The Star-Spangled Banner," which became the National Anthem.

▶ **Crustacean:**
Maryland blue crab
Chesapeake Bay is a major crab-fishing area, and soft-shelled blue crabs that have just molted are a great delicacy.

8

South Carolina

The Palmetto State

Mottos:

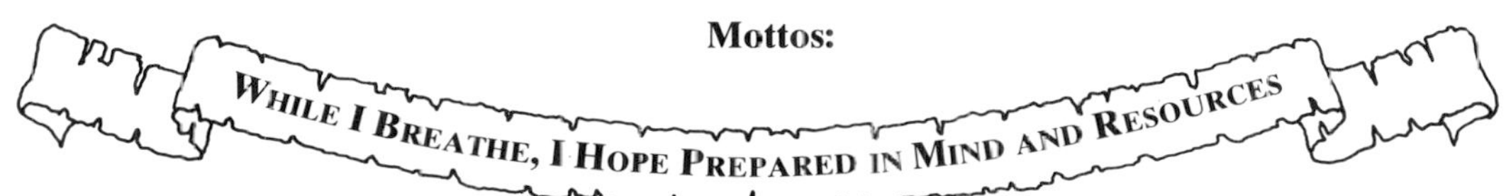

While I Breathe, I Hope
Prepared in Mind and Resources

On May 23 1788 South Carolina became the 8th state. The first permanent settlement was by the English in 1670. Earlier Spanish and French colonies had failed. The Carolinas prospered under colonial rule, but they played a leading role in the Revolution. During the Civil War, almost 15,000 soldiers from the area were killed, and the state suffered great hardship.

After World War II, South Carolina began to prosper and become more industrialized. Tobacco instead of cotton became the main cash crop. Today soybeans, corn, and peaches are also grown. Textile and clothing industries are important, as is furniture making, timber production, and chemicals.

South Carolina is proud of its heritage, and Charleston is noted for its splendid 18th century buildings. Fine beaches, dense woodlands, and rugged mountains also attract tourists. The Blue Ridge Mountains provide the state's most spectacular scenery, with Sassafras Mountain rising to 3,560 feet.

Blue Ridge Mountains
Saluda River
Textiles
GREENVILLE
Logging and furniture making
Tobacco
Georgia
Cotton and textiles
COLUMBIA (capital)
Congaree River
Wateree River
Pee Dee River
Clark Hill Reservoir
Long Bay
Lake Marion
Santee River
Savannah River
Atlantic Ocean
Chemicals
Francis Marion National Forest
CHARLESTON

▼ State flag:
South Carolina added a palmetto tree to the Moultrie flag of 1770 to create their state flag at the time of secession.

▼ Fort Sumter
South Carolina's secession in 1860 and the attack on Fort Sumter in Charleston harbor led directly to the Civil War.

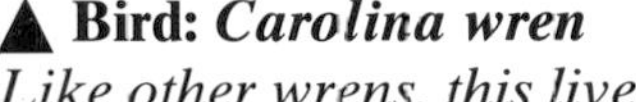

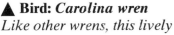

▲ Bird: *Carolina wren*
Like other wrens, this lively little bird has short, rounded wings and a short tail.

◀ Tree: *Cabbage palmetto*
The cabbage, or sabal, palmetto is only found growing wild on the coast. It usually grows 10–20 feet tall and the 6-foot orange flower panicles open in June.

▶ Flower: *Carolina yellow jessamine*
Jessamine is another word for the sweet-smelling jasmine.

9

New Hampshire

The Granite State

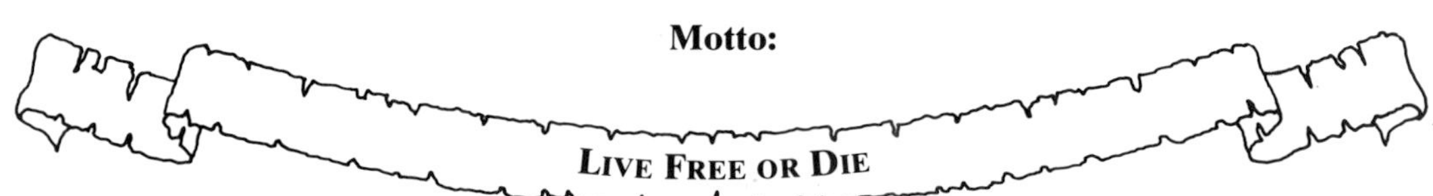

New Hampshire, the 9th state, joined on June 21 1788. It is a very beautiful New England state, with many mountains, green valleys, lakes, rivers, and sandy shores. The winters are very cold, though, and even the summers are cool. There is very little good agricultural land, other than in the valleys of the Merrimack and Connecticut Rivers.

Martin Pring of England was the first explorer, followed by Samuel de Champlain in 1605 and John Smith in 1614. The first settlements were English colonies in 1623 and 1630. Different religious groups fought for control of the area, and Massachusetts and New York squabbled over the borders. In the Revolution its citizens fought bravely, but the state ended up heavily in debt.

Today, there are fewer than one and a half million people in the state. Logging, paper making, electronic goods, traditional textile weaving, and leather work are the main industries. Farming produce includes livestock, poultry, and vegetables. Recreation and tourism are also important.

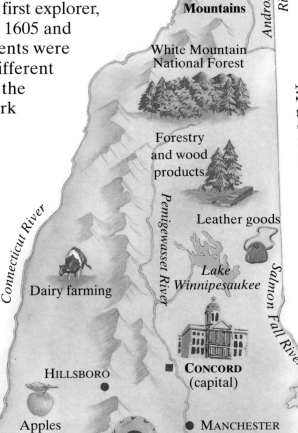

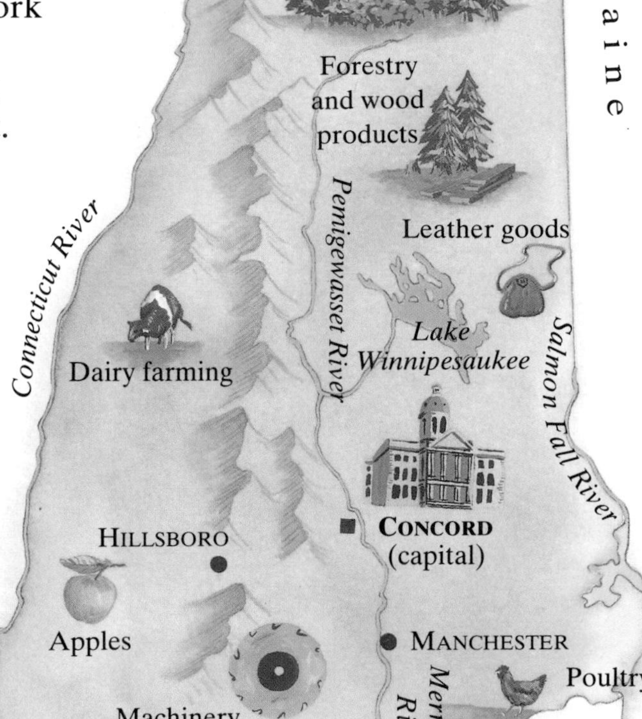

▼ **State flag:**
The nine stars surrounding the state seal show that New Hampshire was the 9th state to join the Union.

▼ **Flower: *Purple lilac***
The sweet-smelling lilac, with its big clusters of flowers, is a member of the olive family.

▼ **Bird: *Purple finch***
The rosy-pink head, back, and breast of the male finch is a distinctive sight in woodlands.

▲ **Tree: *White birch***
The bark of the birch separates into thin, tough layers and is used to make the birch-bark canoe.

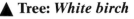

◀ **Westward-ho!**
Concord was a center of the wagon- and coach-building industry and many settlers left for the West in Concord-built vehicles.

Virginia

The Old Dominion

Motto:

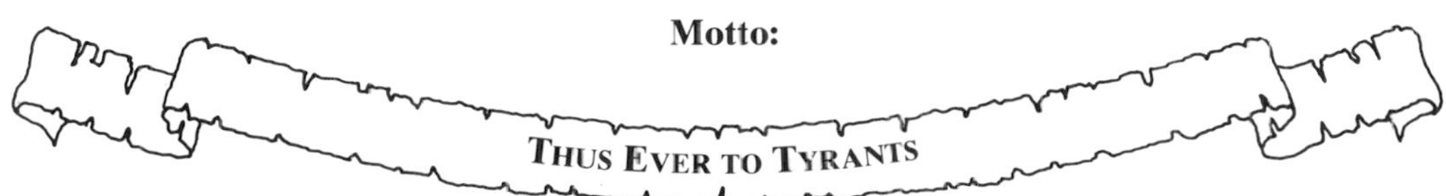

Virginia joined the Union as the 10th state, on June 25 1788. Named for Elizabeth I, the Virgin Queen, Elizabethan colonies of 1585–88 failed. A successful colony was not founded until 1607. After that, settlement was rapid and tobacco farming brought great wealth to Virginia.

In the Revolution, Virginia provided many leaders, including George Washington. In the early days of the republic the state was known as the birthplace of presidents: four of the first five United States presidents came from Virginia. During the Civil War, Richmond was the Confederate capital. The War brought great hardship to the region and recovery was slow.

▲ **State flag:**
In the state seal (1776) Virginia herself tramples a king from whose head the crown has fallen.

▼ **Tobacco**
Tobacco processing is one of the main industries of the area. The quality of Virginian tobacco is famous worldwide.

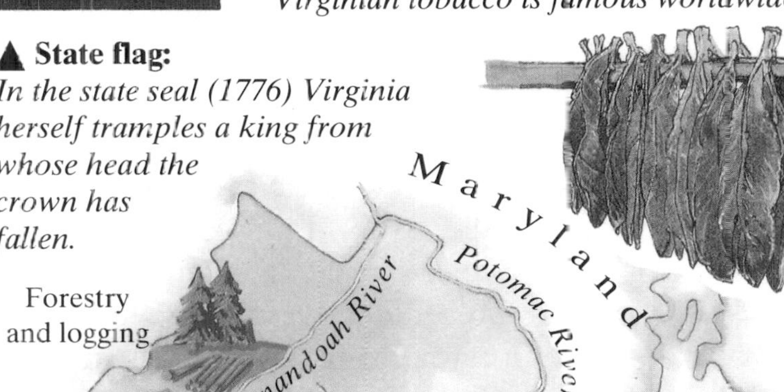

Today, Virginia relies on farming, fishing, mineral resources, and manufacturing. It also provides services for the Federal Government offices in the District of Columbia. Virginia's historical sites and beautiful scenery attract millions of visitors every year.

◀ **Blue Ridge Mountains**
The Blue Ridge Mountains are part of the Appalachian range. Their beautiful forests and abundant wildlife are very popular with tourists.

◀ **Shell: *Oyster***
Oysters were once the food of the poor and the shells were used as material for making roads. Today, they are a symbol of luxury.

▶ **Robert E. Lee**
Robert E. Lee, the great Confederate general, was born in Virginia. His defeat at the Battle of Gettysberg (1863) marked a turning point in the Civil War.

11

New York

The Empire State

Motto:

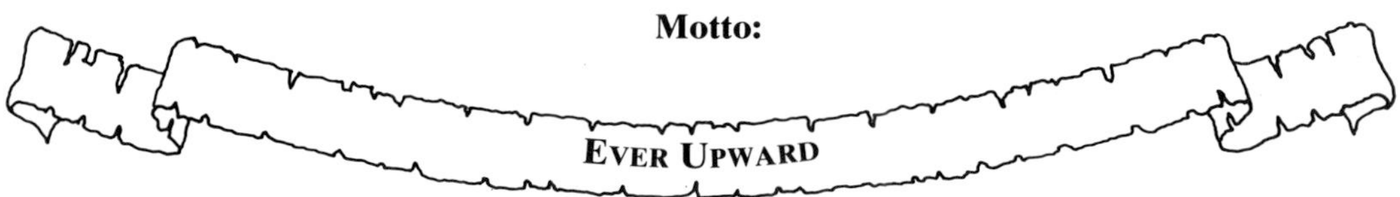

New York became the 11th state, on July 26 1788. Its population and wealth, rivaled today only by California, led to its nickname "The Empire State." The original inhabitants were the Five Indian Nations: Mohawks, Oneidas, Onondagas, Cayugas, and Senecas. Holland claimed the territory in 1610, and founded the city of New Amsterdam on Manhattan Island in 1625. The English arrived in 1664 and, after years of arguments with the Dutch over ownership, the colony became British in 1669. The British renamed the city New York.

The state stretches from the Great Lakes and the Thousand Islands in the north to New York City in the far southeast. The landscape varies from mountains over 5,000 feet high to the low, flat fertile fruit orchards around the Great Lakes. Farming centers on dairy and poultry produce. Industry of all kinds flourishes, and New York is the chief manufacturing state in the country. There are also holiday resorts such as the Adirondacks and the Catskills. The major port of New York City has made the state the commercial, financial, and cultural center of the nation.

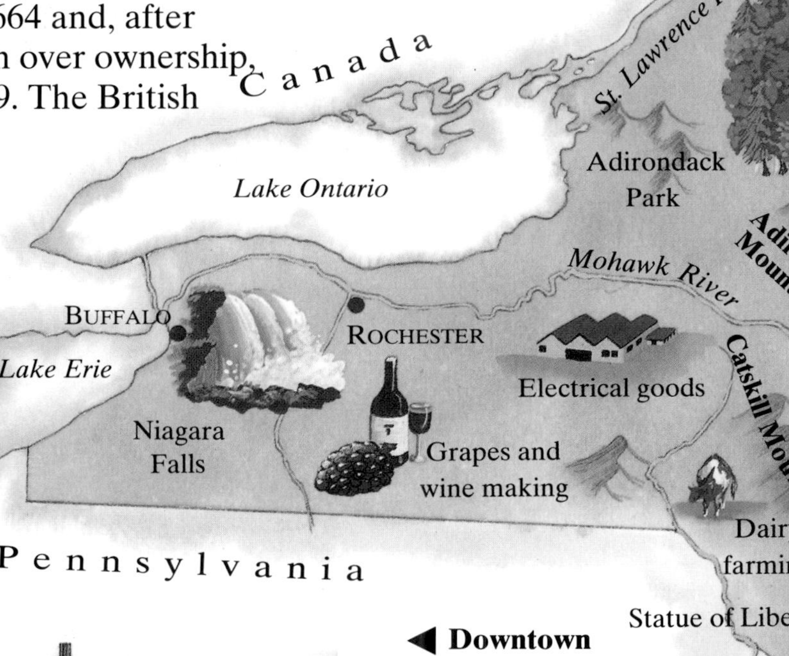

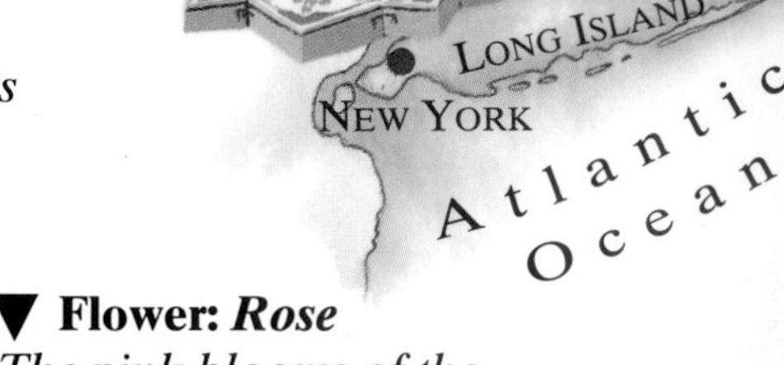

▼ **State flag:**
The state coat of arms and the state motto adorn the New York flag.

◀ **Downtown Manhattan**
Movies have made the Manhattan skyline one of the most familiar sights in the world.

▼ **Tree:** ***Sugar maple***
Maple sugar is made from the sap of this tree, which is also called the hard maple, rock maple or sugar tree.

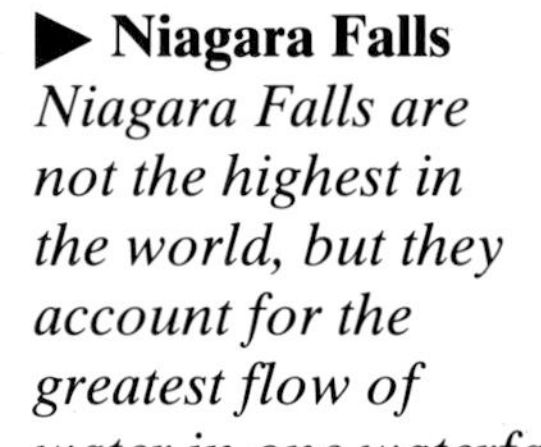

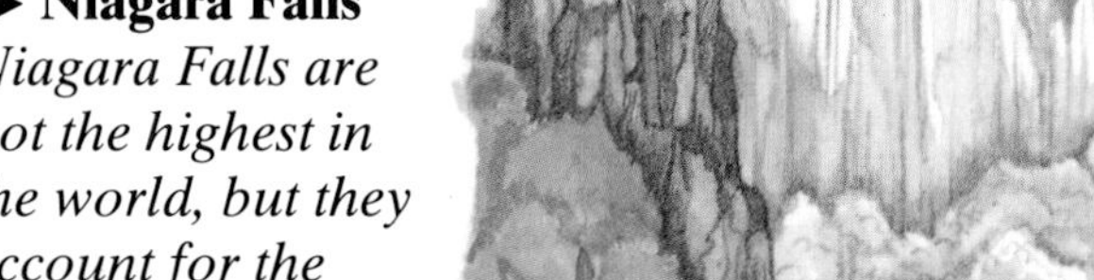

▶ **Niagara Falls**
Niagara Falls are not the highest in the world, but they account for the greatest flow of water in one waterfall.

▼ **Flower:** ***Rose***
The pink blooms of the wild rose appear in early summer and are followed by red hips.

12

North Carolina

The Tar Heel State

Motto:

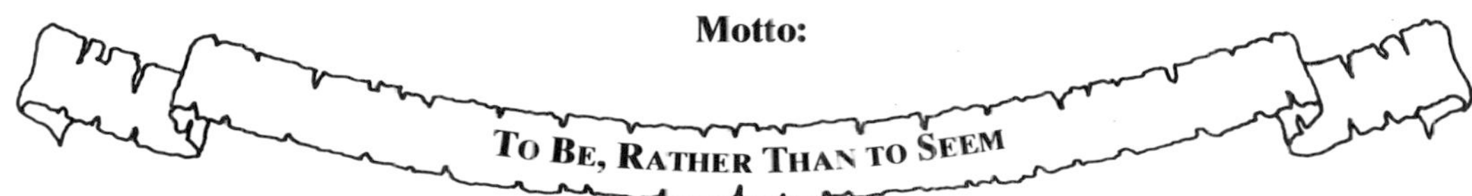
To Be, Rather Than to Seem

North Carolina joined the Union as the 12th state, on November 21 1789. The French and Spanish were the earliest explorers. The British tried unsuccessfully to colonize the area from 1585 to 1590. The first British settlements were founded in 1663. No one knows what happened to the earliest settlers, though some may have been adopted by local tribes. After the Revolution, the state grew so slowly that it was sometimes called the Rip van Winkle State. Eventually cotton and tobacco brought prosperity, but the Civil War left the state with large debts.

Today North Carolina is heavily populated and is the leading industrial state in the south. As well as cotton and textiles, furniture, paper, cigarettes, and processed foods are produced. The main agricultural crops include tobacco, corn, and soybeans. The state has many tourist attractions, including beaches, forests, and mountains. The Great Smokey Mountain National Park, shared with neighboring Tennessee, has 53 peaks more than a mile high.

▶ **State flag:**
The colors and their layout recall the early "Stars and Bars" flag of the Confederacy.

▶ **Flower:** ***Dogwood***
The large white or pink flowers make this a most attractive ornamental shrub.

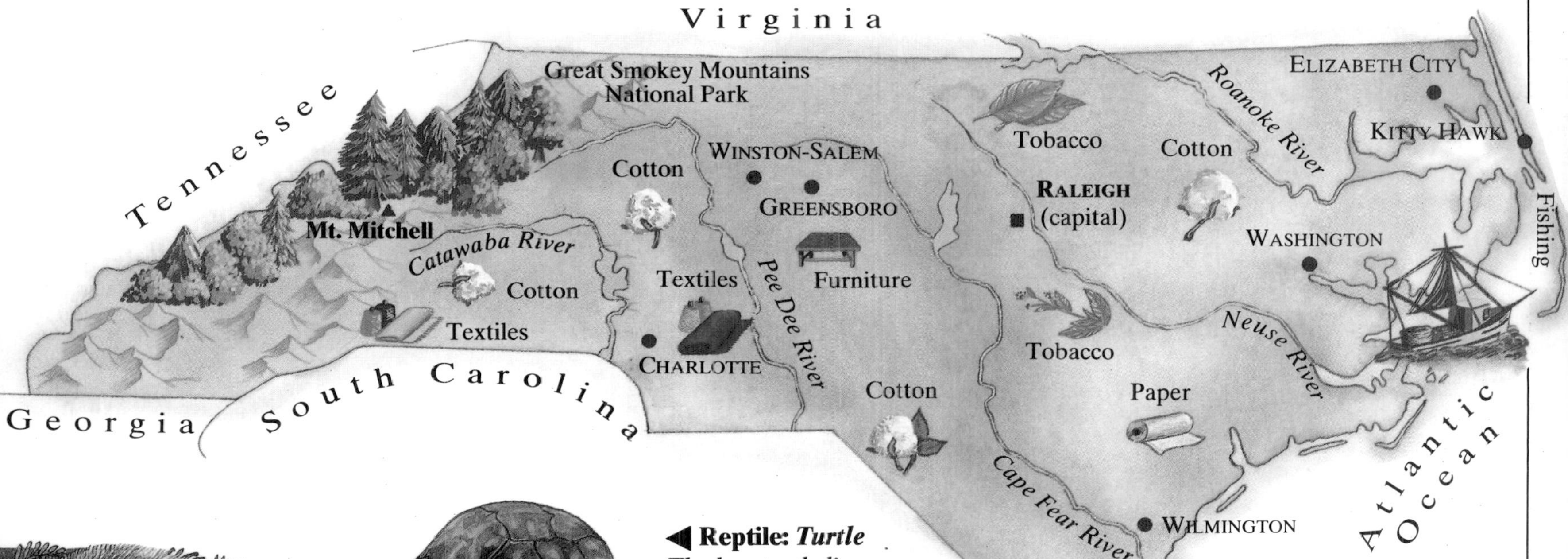

◀ **Reptile:** ***Turtle***
The box turtle lives in wooded areas, feeding on earthworms, insects, and berries.

▼ **Kitty Hawk**
North Carolina license plates say "First in Flight," a reference to the Wright Brothers' first-ever flight at Kitty Hawk.

◀ **Mammal:** ***Gray squirrel***
The gray squirrel lives in forests throughout the United States, feeding on nuts, berries, and buds.

Rhode Island

The Ocean State

Tiny Rhode Island, the smallest state in the Union, was the last of the original 13 states to join, on May 29 1790. Roger Williams established the state in 1636 as a haven from religious persecution in England and the Puritanism of the other states. Although Rhode Island was the first state to declare its independence from England, in May 1776, it did not join the Union until the Bill of Rights was proposed.

For many years Rhode Island's main income came from fishing, ship-building, and trading by sea. Its fast-running streams were harnessed to run textile mills and the state prospered. Rhode Island is still highly industrialized but the cotton mills have been partly replaced by industries manufacturing jewelry, electronics, and machine tools. Agriculture is limited, but the state is famous for its poultry.

This beautiful state has many natural assets — rocky cliffs, sandy beaches, forests, and countless rivers and salt-marshes — and tourism is becoming increasingly important.

▼ State flag:
The anchor and the word "Hope" can be traced back to 1647; the 13 stars stand for the 13 colonies.

▼ Bird: *Rhode Island red*
Developed from Asiatic breeds kept on Rhode Island farms in the 19th century, this distinctive chicken with its red plumage is used for both egg and meat production.

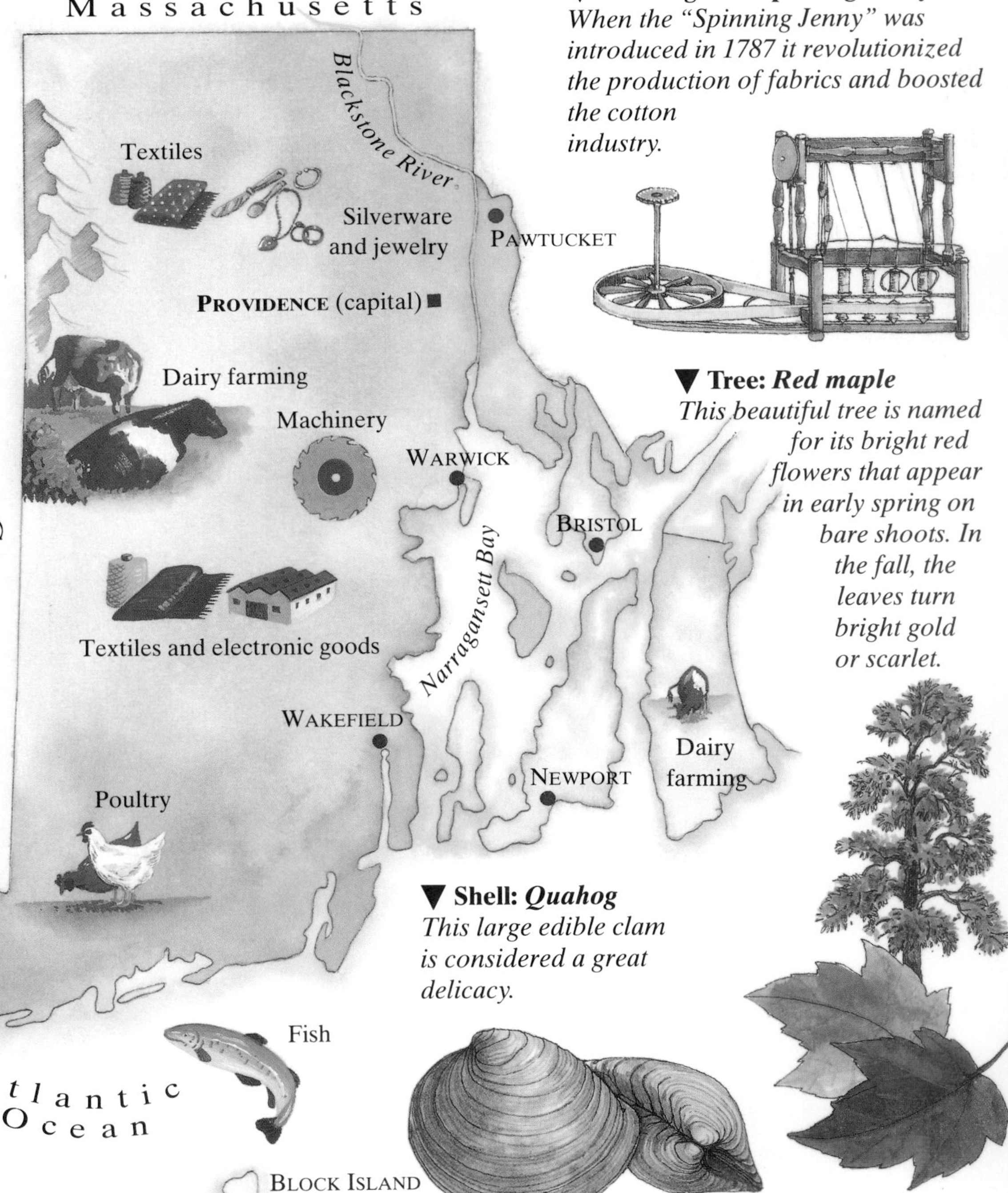

▼ Arkwright's "Spinning Jenny"
When the "Spinning Jenny" was introduced in 1787 it revolutionized the production of fabrics and boosted the cotton industry.

▼ Tree: *Red maple*
This beautiful tree is named for its bright red flowers that appear in early spring on bare shoots. In the fall, the leaves turn bright gold or scarlet.

▼ Shell: *Quahog*
This large edible clam is considered a great delicacy.

14

Vermont

The Green Mountain State

Motto:

Vermont became the 14th state of the Union, on March 4 1791. The area was first explored by the French in 1609. In 1724, permanent Dutch and British settlements opened up the land for colonization. In 1777, an independent state, originally called New Connecticut, was formed. Immigration was rapid over the next 50 years, but in the 1830s many Vermonters moved westward to the new frontiers. Vermont took an active part in the Civil War providing more than 39,000 soldiers to fight on the side of the Union.

Today, Vermont is still sparsely populated with about 600,000 people spread over 9,609 square miles. The main income of this wooded, mountainous state comes from dairy farming, timber, including paper pulp, and marble and granite mines. There are also several small manufacturing industries.

The mountains, woods, and streams that make farming so difficult and unprofitable attract many vacationers. The number of visitors every year often exceeds the total population of the state, making tourism a major industry.

▼ **State flag:**
The state coat of arms shows a landscape with a pine tree, three wheat sheaves, and a cow.

▼ **Bird: *Hermit thrush***
This thrush with its white eye rings is often regarded as the sweetest-singing bird of North America.

▼ **Animal: *Morgan horse***
All Morgan horses alive today descend from one stallion called Justin Morgan (1793–1821).

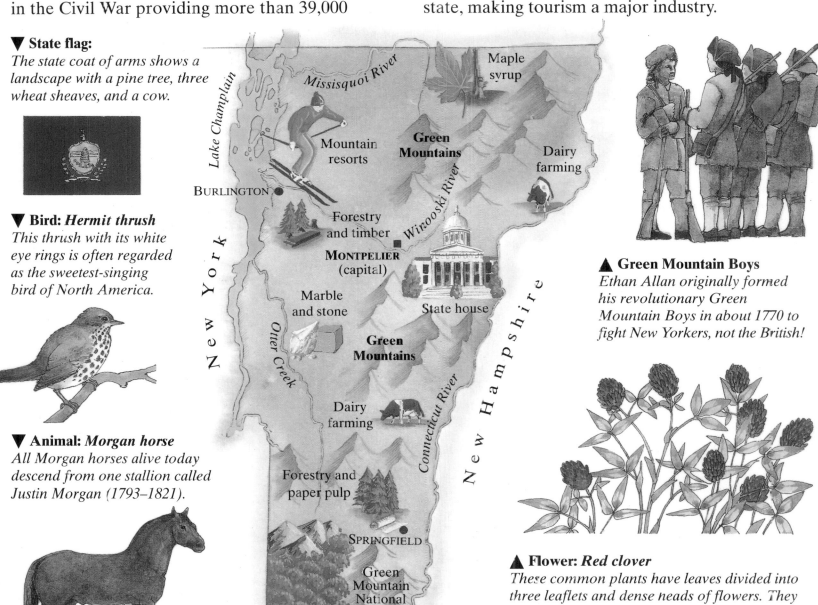

▲ **Green Mountain Boys**
Ethan Allan originally formed his revolutionary Green Mountain Boys in about 1770 to fight New Yorkers, not the British!

▲ **Flower: *Red clover***
These common plants have leaves divided into three leaflets and dense heads of flowers. They are good fodder plants as well as being popular with bees and good for honey production.

Kentucky

The Bluegrass State

Motto:

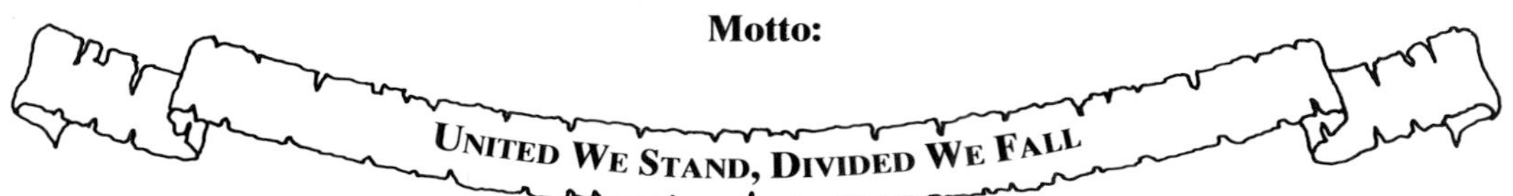

The 15th state to join the Union, on June 1 1792, Kentucky has played an important part in the history of the United States. The region was first colonized by Pennsylvanians during the Revolution. Daniel Boone's Wilderness Road through the Cumberland Gap attracted thousands of settlers. Sometimes whole villages moved from the older states to Kentucky. By 1792 the population was about 75,000. Kentucky's sympathies were divided during the Civil War, which brought much hardship to the area.

Farming has always been important, the main crops being tobacco, corn, hay, and soybeans. Coal mining, although still a major industry, employs fewer people than in the past. Other manufactured goods range from baseball bats and shoelaces to pickles and whiskey. The region is also famous for the breeding of thoroughbred horses and the Kentucky Derby. Many people come to see Kentucky's spectacular scenery, including Mammoth Caves which have more than 150 miles of tunnels, passages, and caverns.

▶ **Kentucky's presidents**
Jefferson Davis and Abraham Lincoln were both born in Kentucky, the only state ever to produce two men who were president at the same time — during the Civil War (1861–65).

▲ **Long rifle**
The famous Kentucky long rifle, much more accurate than the British musket, helped win the Revolution.

▲ **State flag:**
This complicated flag shows many symbols including the state seal (two men shaking hands) and the state motto.

Ohio
Covington
Horses
Big Sandy River
Indiana
Louisville
Frankfort (capital)
Lexington
Agriculture
West Virginia
Coal
Illinois
Owensboro
Ohio River
Fort Knox
Tobacco products
Kentucky River
Oil
Green River
Missouri
National Forest
Mammoth Cave National Park
Coal production
Appalachian Mountains
Virginia
Kentucky Lake
Lake Barkley
Tobacco
Oil
Cumberland River
Tennessee
Middlesboro

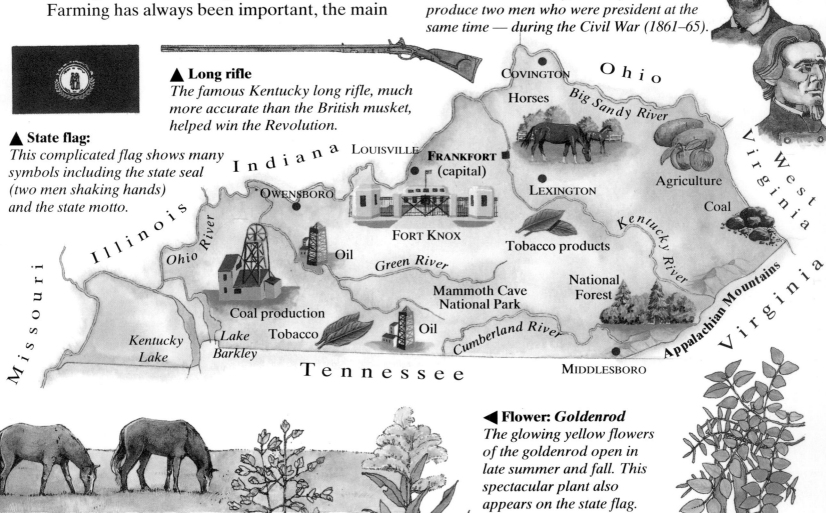

◀ **Flower: *Goldenrod***
The glowing yellow flowers of the goldenrod open in late summer and fall. This spectacular plant also appears on the state flag.

▲▶ **"Blue Grass"**
"Blue Grass" is a common grass of the Kentucky prairies — an area famous for blue grass folk music and racehorses.

▶ **Tree: *Kentucky Coffee Tree***
This is not a real coffee tree at all, but its seeds can be made into a reasonable imitation of coffee.

Tennessee

The Volunteer State

Motto:

Tennessee became the 16th state, on June 1 1796. The land was first explored by Hernando de Soto in 1540 and later by Père Marquette in 1673. The area also formed part of various English royal grants from 1584 onwards. The eastern part of the state was the ancestral hunting ground of many native tribes including the Cherokees, Creeks, and Miamis; the center was Iroquois territory; and Chickasaws lived in the west.

The first white settlements were made between 1768 and 1780. By 1795 there were more than the 60,000 settlers required for statehood. In the Civil War, Tennessee was a major battleground.

Today, Tennessee is highly industrialized and the largest producer of zinc and electricity in the country. Aluminum refining, using hydroelectric power from the Tennessee Valley Authority, is a major industry. Agriculture is limited but cotton and tobacco remain important crops.

Country and western music is now big business and its center is at Nashville. The stunning mountain scenery encourages further tourism.

▼ **State flag:**
Tennessee was the third state to join the Union after the thirteen original colonies: hence the three stars.

◀ **Animal:** ***Raccoon***
The raccoon has a distinctive masklike black patch across the eyes and a striped tail. It forages at night, feeding on anything it can find from roots to garbage.

▶ **Horse:** ***Tennessee walking horse***
Allen, a stallion that lived at the beginning of the 20th century, was the ancestor of all the Tennessee walking horses alive today.

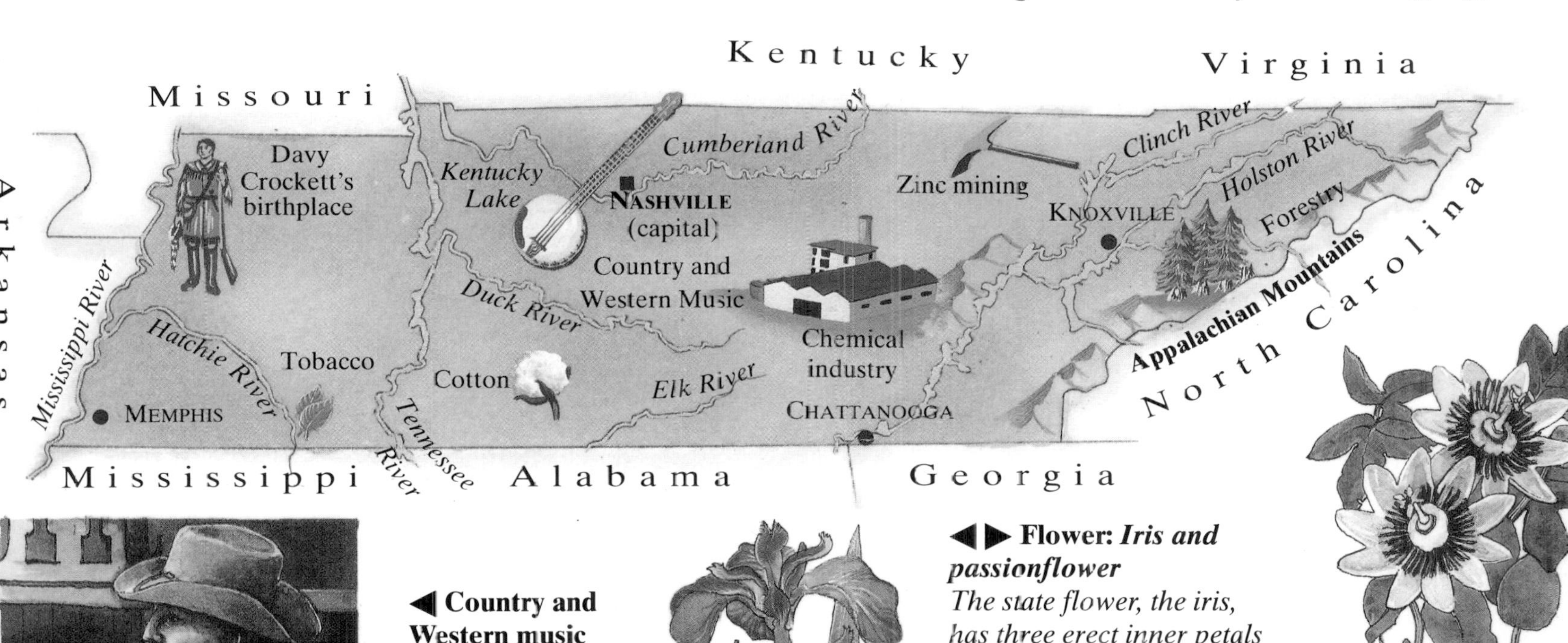

◀ **Country and Western music**
Country and western music is for ever associated with Tennessee. The Grand Ole Opry is in Nashville.

◀▶ **Flower:** ***Iris and passionflower***
The state flower, the iris, has three erect inner petals and three drooping outer sepals. The beautiful state wildflower, the passionflower, develops large orange-colored fruits in the fall.

17

Ohio

The Buckeye State

Motto:

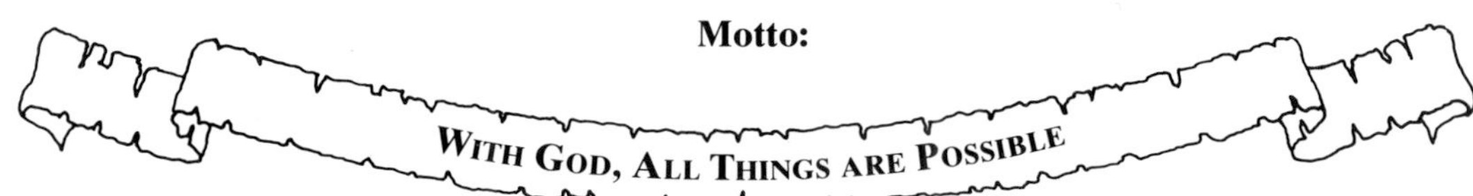

Ohio became the 17th state, on March 1 1803. The area was first explored in the late 1600s, when the French and British disputed ownership. Ohio became British territory in 1763 and finally came under US control in 1783 as part of the Northwest Territory. The state was first opened up by river traffic on the Ohio River in the early 1800s. Steamboats followed in the 1820s, and then came the National Road from West Virginia to Indiana in 1833. This east-west travel route was one of the keys to Ohio's rapid growth. By the 1850s there were over 2,000,000 residents.

Ohio is a major manufacturer of iron and steel, glass, and automobiles. Almost three-quarters of the population live or work in cities, although over half of Ohio is farmland producing wool, corn, pork, and dairy goods. Ohio also exploits its many mineral resources, including coal, natural gas, oil, clay, and stone.

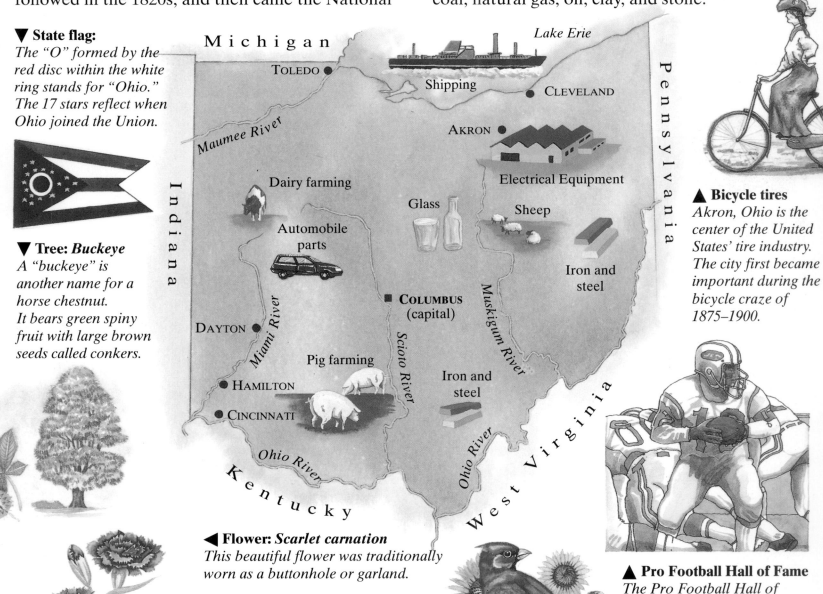

▼ **State flag:**
The "O" formed by the red disc within the white ring stands for "Ohio." The 17 stars reflect when Ohio joined the Union.

▼ **Tree: *Buckeye***
A "buckeye" is another name for a horse chestnut. It bears green spiny fruit with large brown seeds called conkers.

Michigan
Lake Erie
Toledo
Shipping
Cleveland
Pennsylvania
Maumee River
Akron
Electrical Equipment
Indiana
Dairy farming
Glass
Sheep
Automobile parts
Iron and steel
Columbus (capital)
Muskigum River
Dayton
Miami River
Scioto River
Pig farming
Iron and steel
Hamilton
Cincinnati
West Virginia
Ohio River
Ohio River
Kentucky

▲ **Bicycle tires**
Akron, Ohio is the center of the United States' tire industry. The city first became important during the bicycle craze of 1875–1900.

◀ **Flower: *Scarlet carnation***
This beautiful flower was traditionally worn as a buttonhole or garland.

▶ **Bird: *Red cardinal***
The male's red body and black "face" and bib make it instantly recognizable.

▲ **Pro Football Hall of Fame**
The Pro Football Hall of Fame, the ultimate accolade for professional players, is in Canton, Ohio.

18

Louisiana

The Pelican State

Motto:

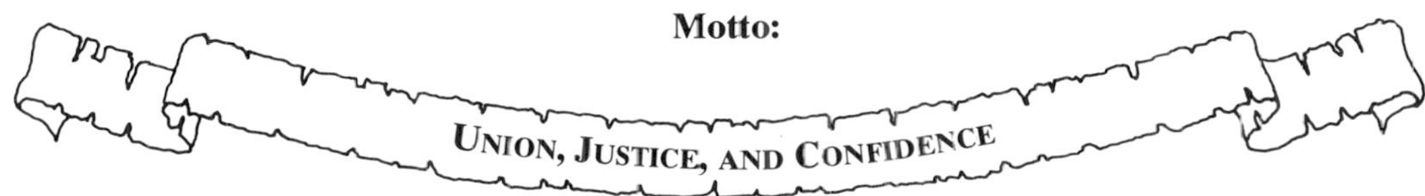

The 18th state to join the Union, on April 30 1812, Louisiana is unique because it still retains the flavor of its French settlers. The first European explorers were Spanish, but several Native American tribes had occupied the land for thousands of years. In 1682, Robert Cavelier claimed the area for France, naming it Louisiana in honor of Louis XIV. In 1762 a secret treaty handed Louisiana over to Spain. It remained under European control until 1803, when the United States bought the state as part of the Louisiana Purchase.

If the French set the style for the culture, the land itself has its own style. Even the highest parts of the state are only just over 500 feet above sea level. The land is so damp and swampy in places that traditional Louisiana graveyards contain brick-built tombs that hold the coffins *above* ground level.

Louisiana is still largely agricultural and many crops grow well in the fertile soil including soybeans, cotton, sugarcane, rice, corn, and timber. Industry is expanding, however, and there are also large deposits of oil, mostly in the south.

▼ **State flag:**
The state flag combines the state's motto with its bird.

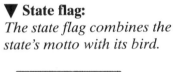

▼ **Bird: *Pelican (Eastern brown)***
This coastal seabird, the smallest New World pelican, is an endangered species.

▶ **Crustacean: *Crawfish***
The crawfish is an essential ingredient in many Cajun dishes.

Arkansas
Soybean
Corn
SHREVEPORT
Driskill Mountain
Timber
Cotton
Red River
Sugarcane
Mississippi River
Mississippi
Texas
Sabine River
Cattle
Rice
Lake Charles
Salt
Jazz
BATON ROUGE (capital)
Oil
NEW ORLEANS
Swamps
Gulf of Mexico

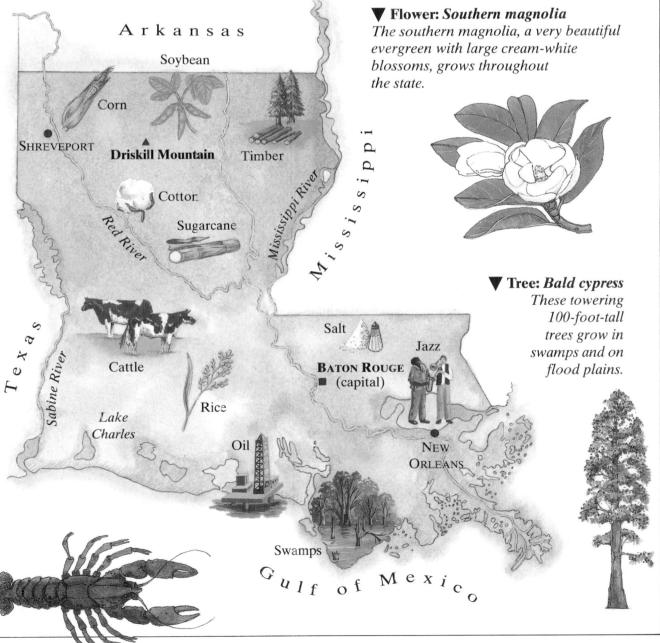

▼ **Flower: *Southern magnolia***
The southern magnolia, a very beautiful evergreen with large cream-white blossoms, grows throughout the state.

▼ **Tree: *Bald cypress***
These towering 100-foot-tall trees grow in swamps and on flood plains.

Indiana

The Hoosier State

Motto:

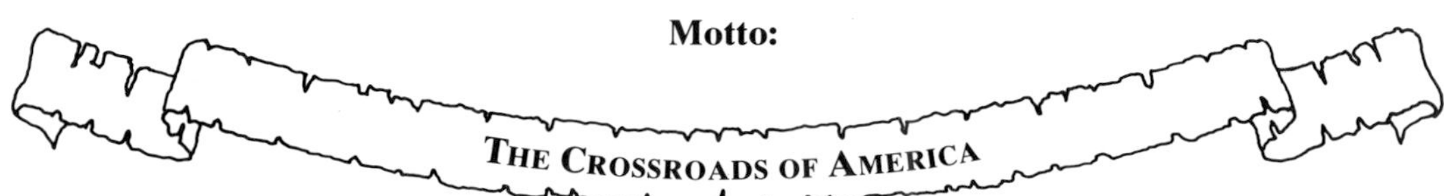

Indiana became the 19th state, on December 11 1816, after a lively history. The French settlement at Vincennes (1732) was the only permanent European settlement until after the Revolution. The state was controlled in turn by the French, the British, and the American revolutionaries. Until 1811 there were constant Indian wars, ending in the defeat of Tecumseh at Tippecanoe. After 1812, many more settlers came and Indiana became a state.

The Great Lakes gave easy access to Indiana and aided transport of goods. Industry soon became established alongside the traditional farming of corn, wheat, and hogs. All kinds of things are, or have been, manufactured in Indiana: musical instruments and mobile homes in Elkhart, plastic and food in Terre Haute, and bottles and furniture in Muncie. In spite of the state's rural image and the fact that three-quarters of it is still farmland, industry employs many more people than agriculture. Indiana's many state parks and recreation facilities attract thousands of tourists.

▼ **State flag:**
The torch symbolizes liberty; the thirteen outer stars are the original colonies; the large star is Indiana; and the other five stars are the rest of the states.

▼ **Tree: *Tulip tree***
A relative of the magnolia, the primitive tulip tree has greenish tulip-shaped flowers.

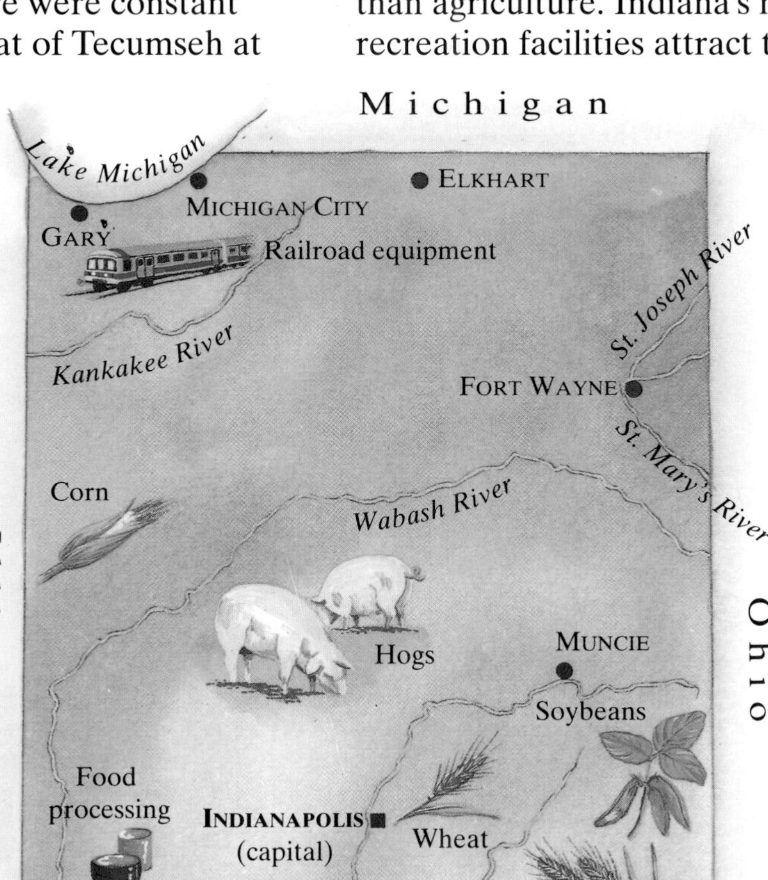

▼ **Flower: *Peony***
The showy pink flowers of this large shrub open in early summer.

▼ **"Indy cars"**
Indianapolis, home of the "Indy 500," is known to motor racing fans the world over. "Indy cars" frequently exceed 200 mph.

▼ **Early explorers**
The first European explorers were French fur traders and Jesuit missionaries, often traveling by birch-bark canoe.

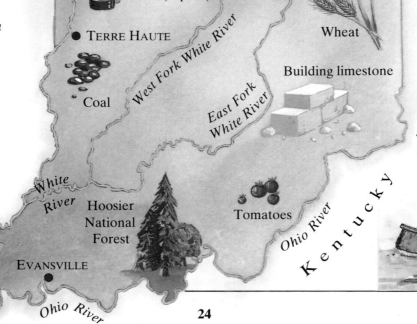

Mississippi

The Magnolia State

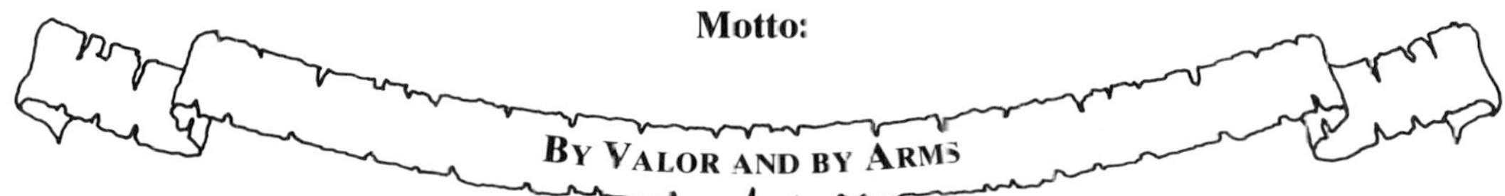

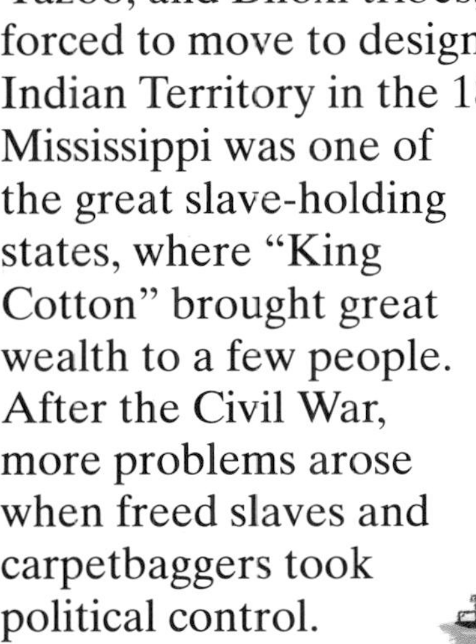

Mississippi became the 20th state of the Union, on December 10 1817. The Spanish explored the area in 1540, but soon left. In 1699 the French settled at Biloxi Bay. They ruled the region until 1763. It then became British territory. During the Revolution, Spain took over once again, ruling until 1798. The area had been home to the Pascagoula, Choctaw, Chickasaw, Natchez, Yazoo, and Biloxi tribes, but they were forced to move to designated Indian Territory in the 1820s. Mississippi was one of the great slave-holding states, where "King Cotton" brought great wealth to a few people. After the Civil War, more problems arose when freed slaves and carpetbaggers took political control.

Since then, Mississippi has slowly prospered. Its rich lowlands — the highest point in the state is only about 800 feet — are ideal for cotton and other agriculture. Natural gas and oil are of increasing importance. Manufacturing of ships, textiles, timber products, and chemicals are the main industries.

▼ Tree and flower: *Southern magnolia*
Mississippi is fiercely proud of its Southern heritage, of which magnolias are an essential part. At up to 10 inches across, the flowers are the biggest of any native tree.

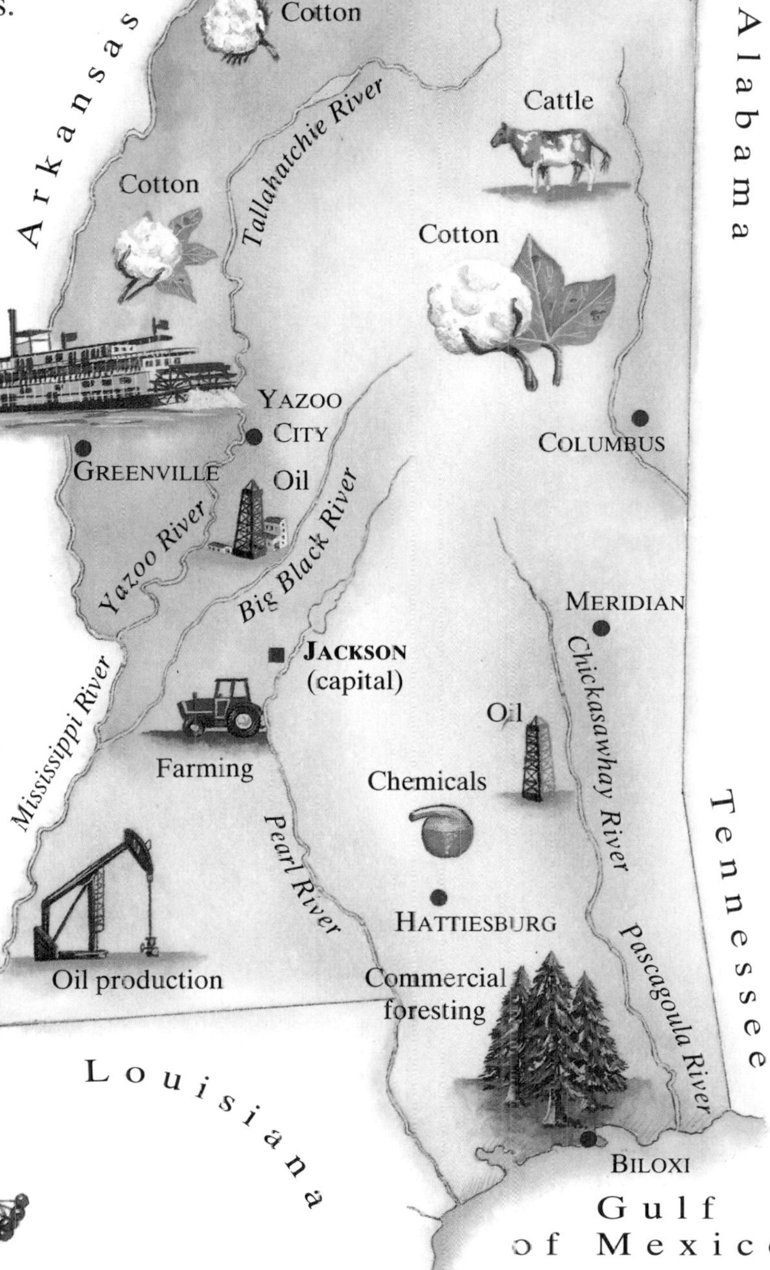

▼ "Old man river"
The mighty Mississippi is the greatest inland waterway of the United States. Its river-boats were very important in opening up the country.

▲ State flag:
The red, white, and blue stripes, after French rule, are combined with the Confederate Battle Flag.

▼ Bird: Mockingbird
Like the magnolia, the mockingbird, a superb mimic, is a traditional symbol of the Ante-Bellum (pre-war) South.

▶ "Carpetbaggers"
"Carpetbaggers" were profiteers who came down from the North with their possessions in carpet-bags.

Illinois

The Prairie State

Motto:

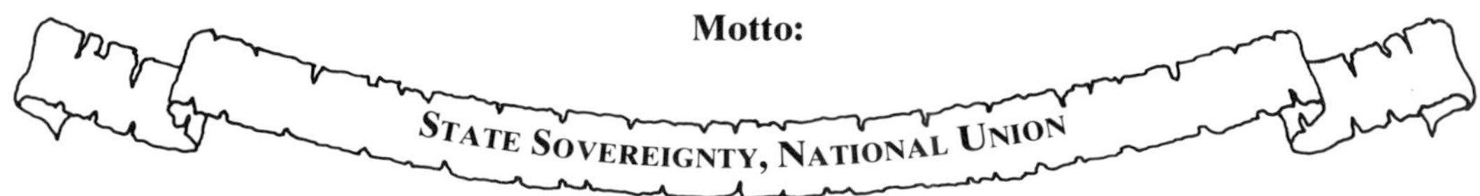

On December 3 1818, Illinois became the 21st state to join the Union. French explorers visited the area in 1659, and the first settlements were French. The Treaty of Paris in 1763 handed control over to the British, but the local Native Americans and the French resisted. The British did not take possession until 1765. In 1778, the Americans captured the British seat of government and Illinois became a county of Virginia. When the Northwest Territory was divided, Illinois became part of Indiana. It finally achieved separate statehood in 1809.

Today, Illinois lives mainly by farming (corn, soybeans, and pigs) and food processing. There is also a wide range of industries including the production of fabricated metal and electrical goods, printing, and publishing. The most famous industrial city is Chicago, which is one of the leading centers for the arts in America. Although there are few wilderness areas left, there are many lakes and streams to attract visitors.

◀ **State flag:**
The state motto held within the eagle's bill is a combination of states' rights and federalism.

▶ **Insect: *Monarch butterfly***
The Monarch spends the summer in the northern United States and the winter in California, Florida, and Mexico.

▼ **Animal: *White-tailed deer***
The flash of this elegant animal's white rump as it flees from danger acts as a warning to other deer.

▶ **Flower: *Violet***
These shade-loving plants have guidelines on their petals to lead insects to the pollen at their center.

▶ **Honest Abe**
Illinois is known as the "Land of Lincoln." Although Lincoln was born in Kentucky, it was in Illinois that he made his mark.

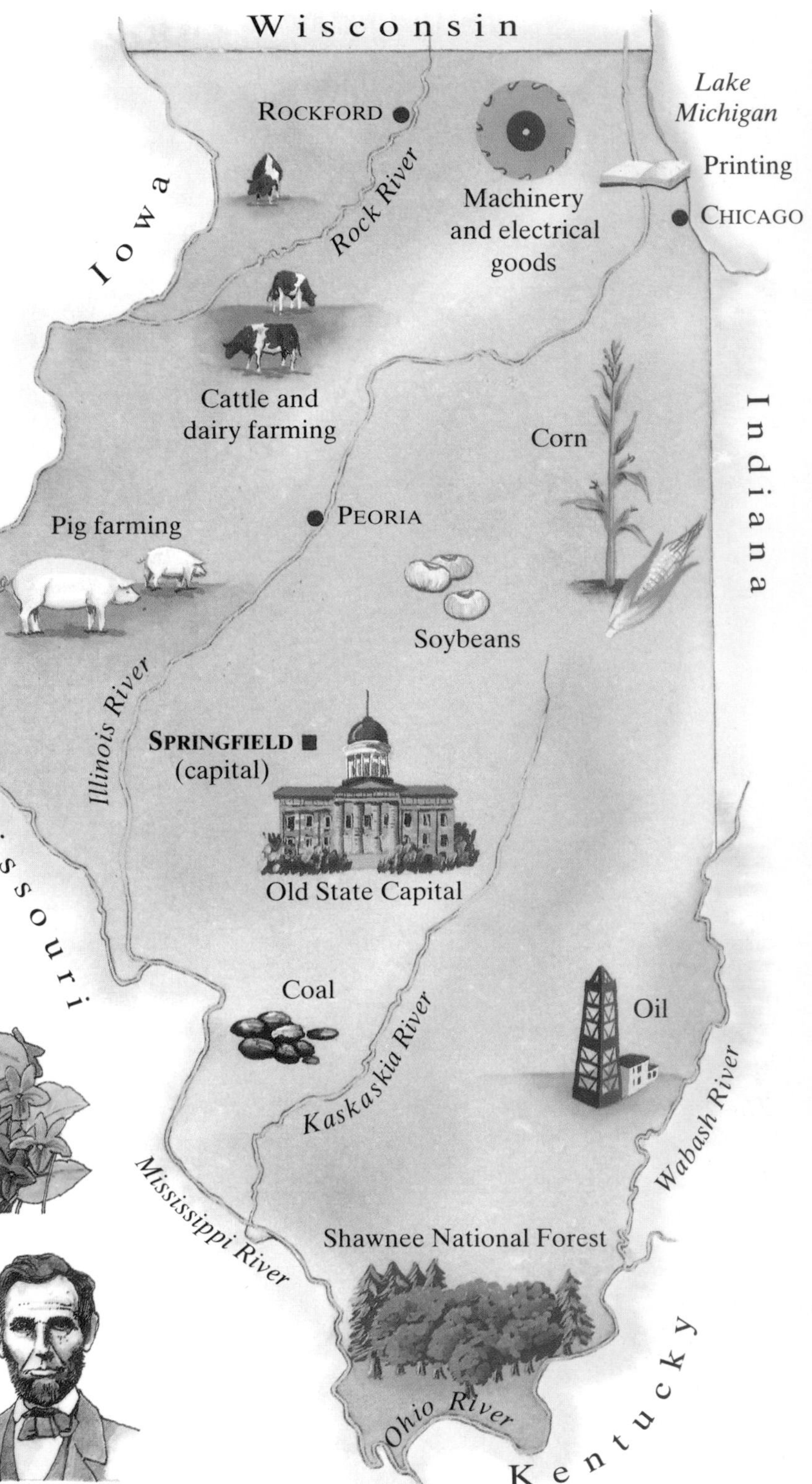

Alabama

The Yellowhammer State

Motto:

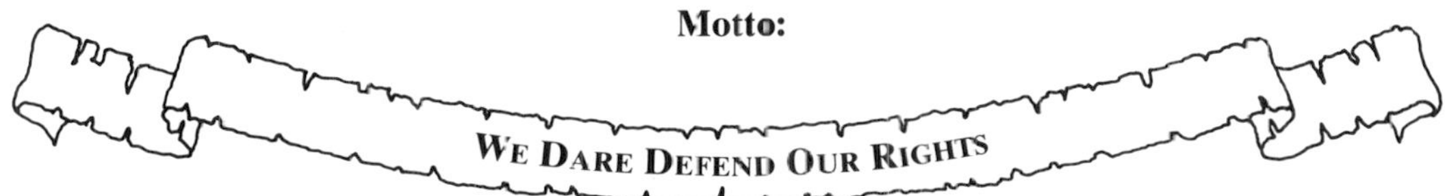

Alabama was admitted to the Union as the 22nd state, on December 14 1819. The Spanish explored the area in 1540, building a fort at Mobile Bay in 1559.The French followed in 1701, with a settlement at Fort Louis. Decades of wars with the British ended in 1763 when the Treaty of Paris awarded the area to Britain. In 1783, American control was recognized.

Alabama has always been a traditional Southern state. The first White House of the Confederacy was in Montgomery. Originally the area was home to many local tribes including the Creek, Choctaw, Chickasaw, and Cherokee. They ceded their lands to the Americans and were moved to western territories.

Lush and green, Alabama has always been a farming state. Once famous for its cotton, its main crops are now corn, peanuts, and timber. Cattle farming is also increasing. Fishing is important on the Gulf Coast, and coal, iron, and oil are also produced. Although one of the poorest states economically, it has a rich rural culture.

▶ **State flag:**
The state flag is the Saltire of St Patrick, either in honor of Irish and Scottish settlers or taken from the Confederate Battle Flag.

▲ **Bird: *Wild turkey***
Once widespread, these large ground birds are now harder to find. They are still popular game birds in Alabama.

▼ **Tree: *Southern pine***
The longleaf or southern pine grows up to 120 feet tall with 10–16 inch needles and large (8–10 inch) cones.

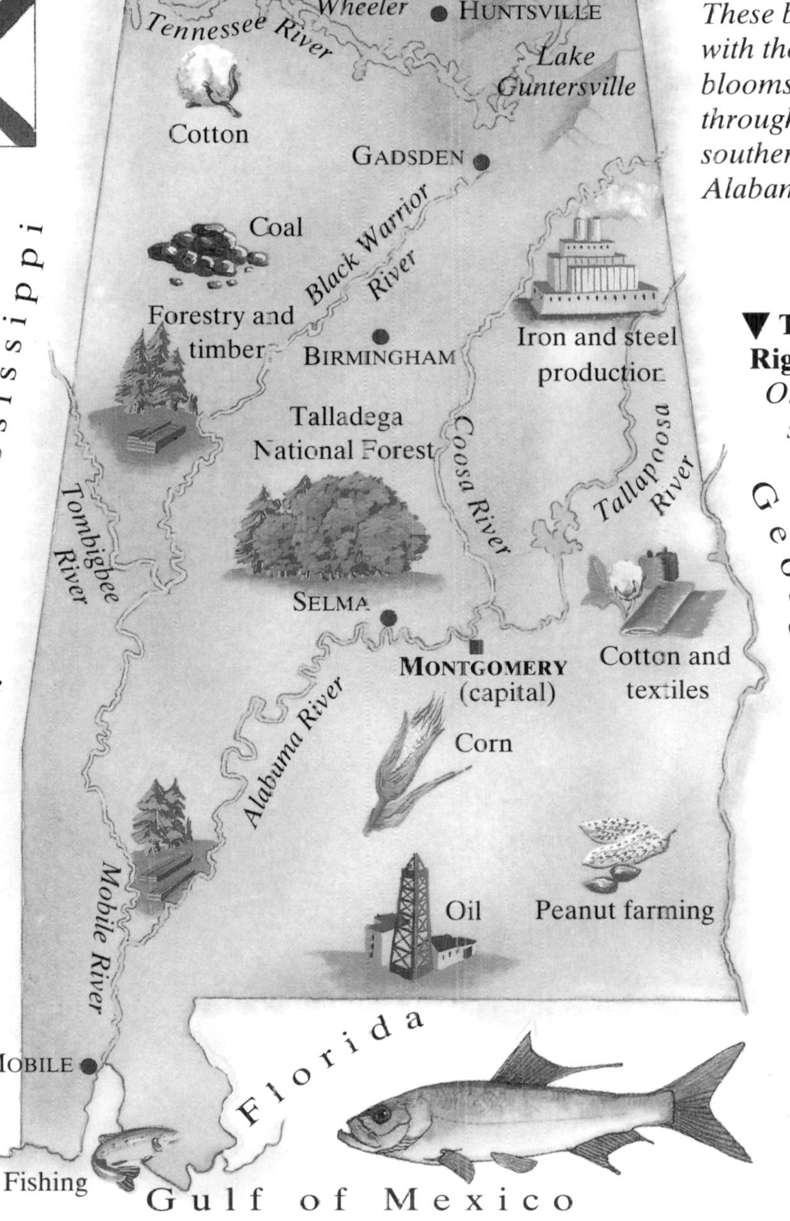

▼ **Flower: *Camellia***
These beautiful shrubs with their showy blooms grow throughout southern Alabama.

▼ **The Civil Rights movement**
One of the great success stories of modern America, this movement is strongly associated with Selma, Alabama.

◀ **Fish: *Tarpon***
This magnificent game fish is found in the Gulf.

Maine

The Pine Tree State

Maine joined the Union as the 23rd state, on March 15 1820. John Cabot explored the area in 1497, only five years after Columbus. The English and French both claimed the area in the early 1600s. Disputes continued until 1763 when the British took control. At first, Maine was a part of Massachusetts, but after the War of 1812 most people wanted separate statehood. In 1820, Congress formed the new state of Maine.

For most of the 19th century, Maine was the principal ship-building state of the Union, making "wooden walls" of all sizes. The other traditional industry is fishing. Wood products, and dairy and fruit farming are also important. Much of Maine is made up of the peaks of a submerged mountain range, separated by a network of rivers, lakes, and waterways. The area attracts many tourists, who come for the beautiful scenery, local culture, and to enjoy the outdoor life.

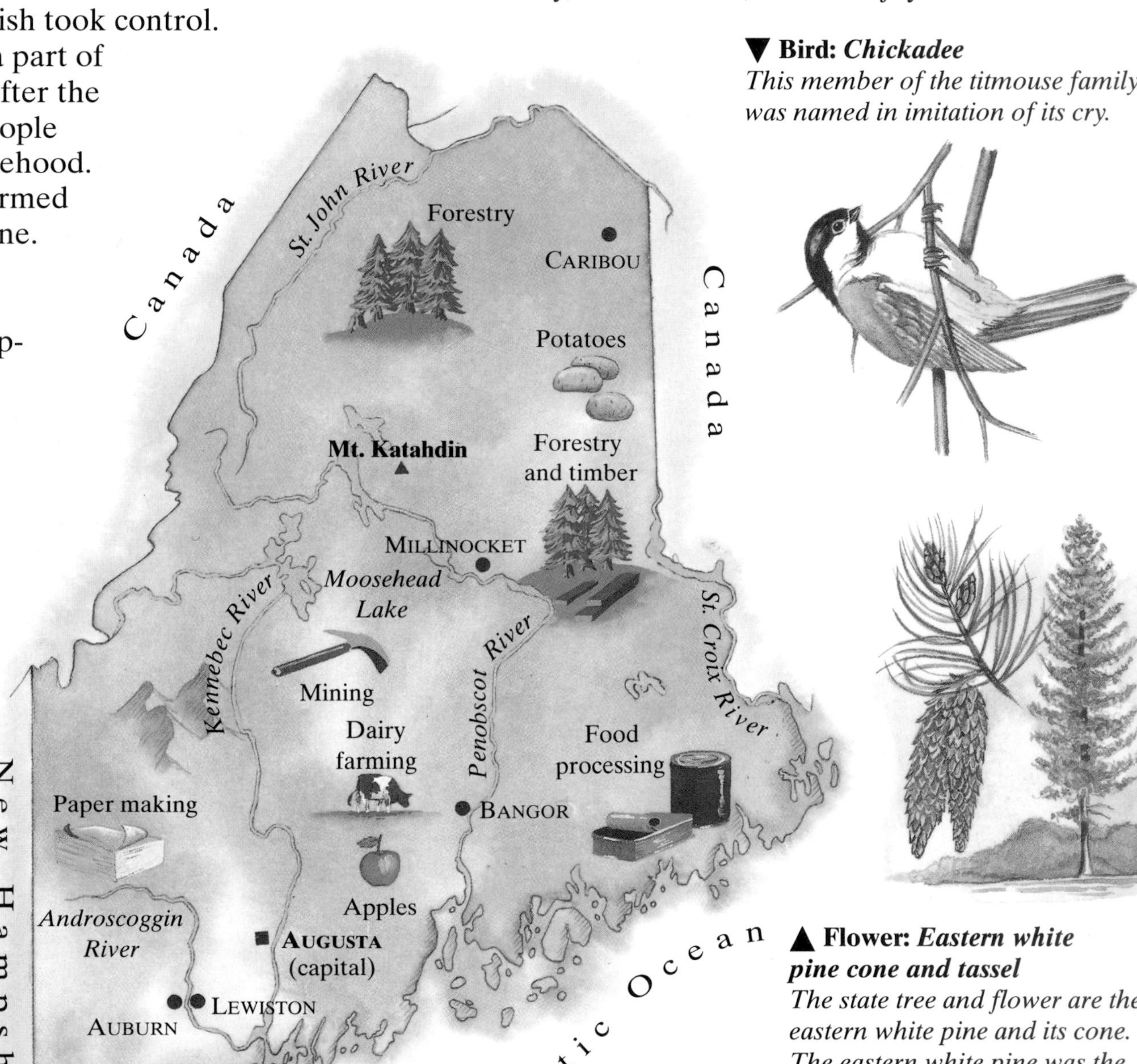

▼ **Bird:** ***Chickadee***
This member of the titmouse family was named in imitation of its cry.

▼ **State flag:**
The state seal shows a moose lying under a pine tree, with a farmer on one side and a sailor on the other.

▼ **Mineral:**
Tourmaline
This semi-precious gemstone can be cut and polished to make attractive jewelry.

▲ **Flower:** ***Eastern white pine cone and tassel***
The state tree and flower are the eastern white pine and its cone. The eastern white pine was the most important timber tree in America in the 19th century.

◀ **Sea-food**
Maine's sea-food is famous, especially Maine lobster.

Missouri

The Show-Me State

Motto:

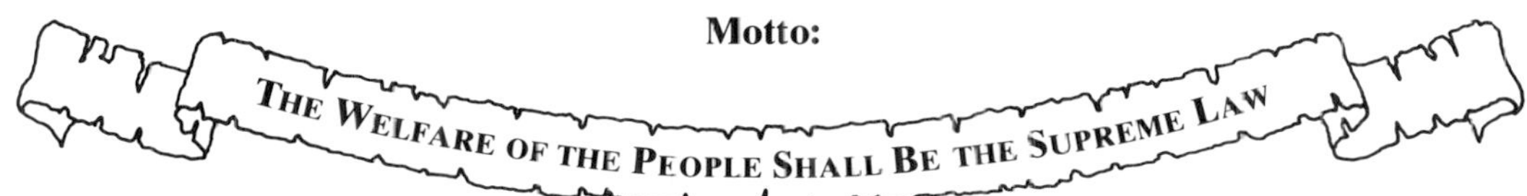

On August 10 1821, Missouri became the 24th state of the Union, 17 years after the United States flag was first hoisted in St. Louis in 1804. The first permanent settlement was by the French at St. Genevieve in 1735 and St. Louis was founded in 1764. After the Revolution, immigrants from many other states arrived, but most of the residents were still French. America bought Missouri as part of the Louisiana Purchase of 1803. From 1815 to 1860, Missouri was frontier territory as the nation pressed westwards. There were few settlers in the Ozarks even in the 1860s, but later people from neighboring Kentucky settled there.

Divided by the Missouri River, the state has fertile prairies and rolling hills in the north and west, and the forested Ozark Plateau in the south. General farming and livestock can be found on the plains, and the traditional crops are soybeans, corn, wheat, and oats. Missouri also has lead, iron, and limestone mines. Manufacturing of transport equipment, food products, and chemicals are the main industries.

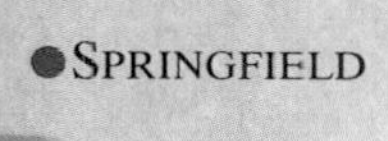

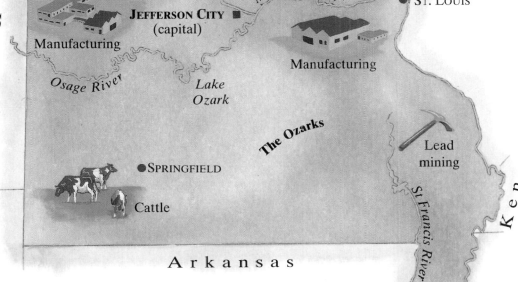

▶ **State flag:**
The arms of Missouri appear inside a ring of 24 stars, Missouri being the 24th state.

▼ **Bird: *Bluebird***
The eastern bluebird is about 6–7 inches long with a blue back and red-brown breast.

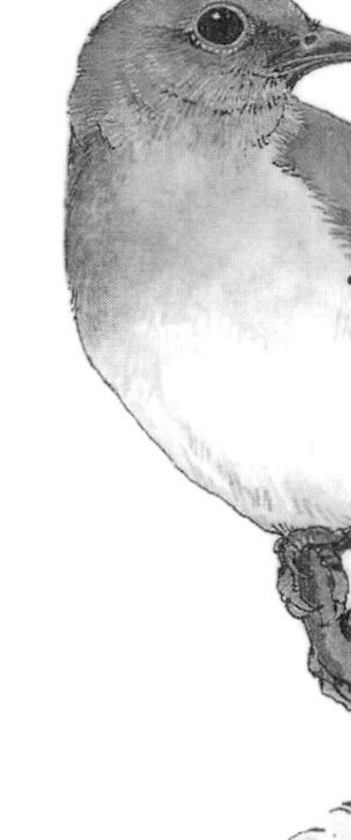

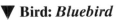

◀ **Pony Express**
The famous Pony Express operated only from 1860–61, until the telegraph was completed. It must have been the most dramatic mail service ever.

▶ **Mark Twain**
Hannibal, on the Mississippi, was the boyhood home of Samuel Clemens (1835–1910) better known as the writer Mark Twain.

25

Arkansas

Land of Opportunity

Motto:

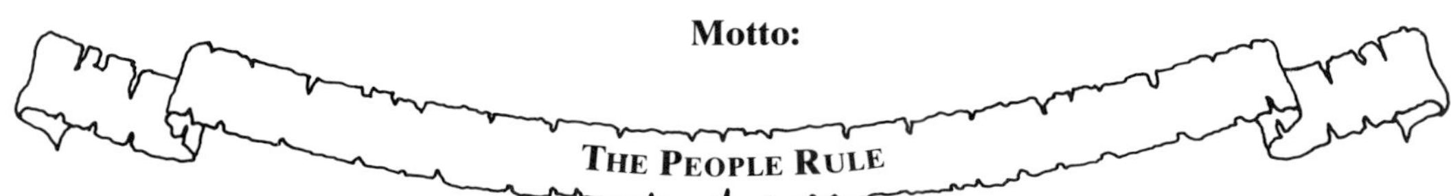

Arkansas became the 25th state of the Union, on June 15 1836. The area was first explored by the Spanish and French in the 1500s and 1600s, though pre-Columbian settlements had flourished at least a thousand years earlier. The first European settlement in 1686 was French, under Henri de Tonti. In 1803 the region was bought by the United States as part of the Louisiana Purchase. Arkansas remained within Louisiana until 1812 and then became part of Missouri. Finally, in 1819 it became Arkansas Territory.

The state has many natural assets. The Arkansas River Valley, which divides the forested Ozarks from the Ouachita Mountains, is an industrial area. There is general farming in the northwest, and cotton, soybeans, and rice grow in the east. The southwest has oil and large cattle ranches. The famous hot springs and National Forests are great tourist attractions.

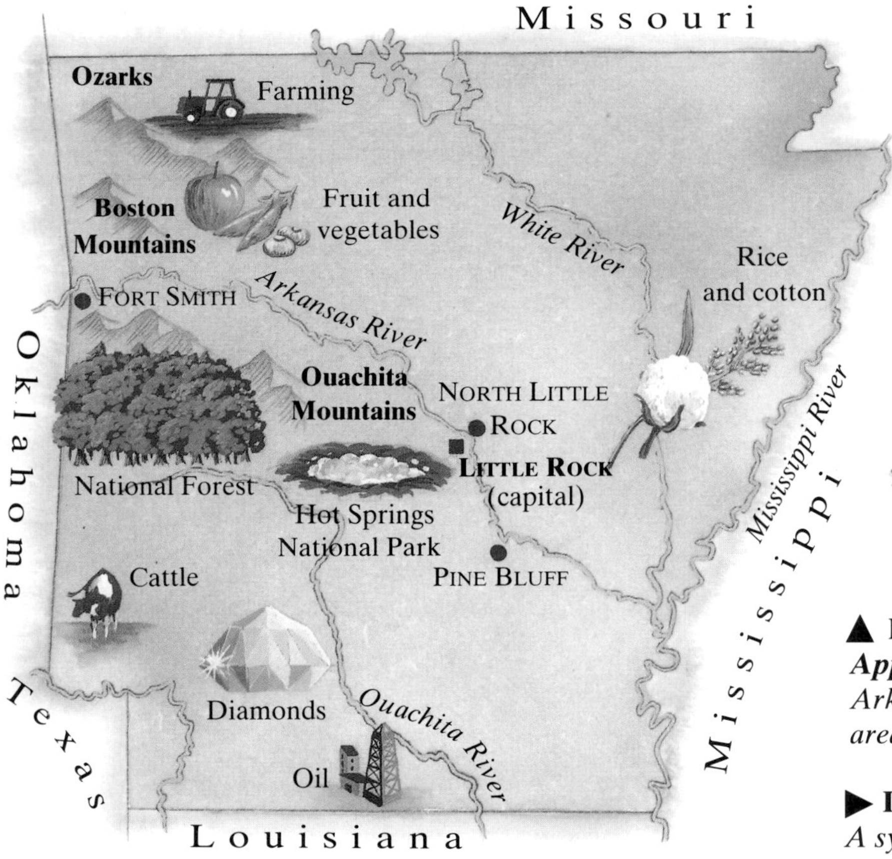

Missouri
Ozarks
Farming
Boston Mountains
Fruit and vegetables
White River
Rice and cotton
FORT SMITH
Arkansas River
Oklahoma
Ouachita Mountains
NORTH LITTLE ROCK
LITTLE ROCK (capital)
National Forest
Hot Springs National Park
Mississippi River
Mississippi
Cattle
PINE BLUFF
Texas
Diamonds
Ouachita River
Oil
Louisiana

◀ **State flag:** *The star above "Arkansas" stands for the Confederacy. The three stars below stand for France, Spain, and the United States. The 25 stars stand for its position as the 25th state.*

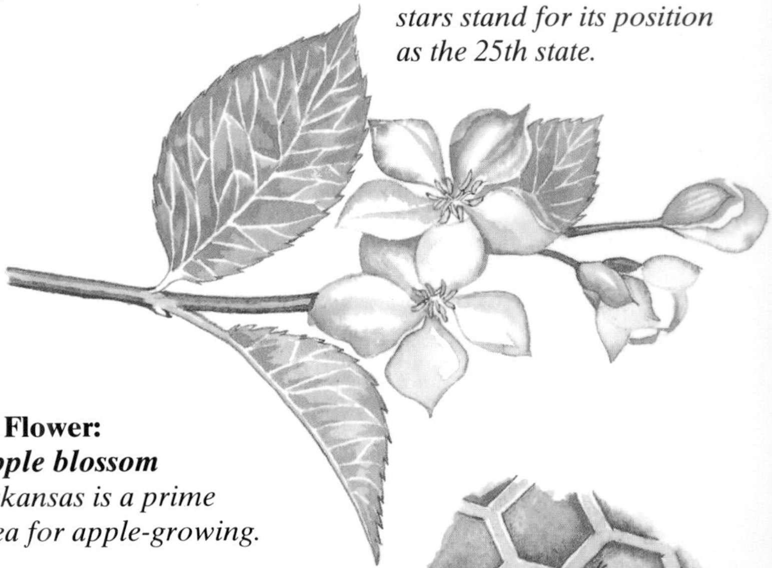

ARKANSAS

▲ **Flower: *Apple blossom*** *Arkansas is a prime area for apple-growing.*

▶ **Insect: *Honeybee*** *A symbol of industry, the honeybee is kept in hives throughout the state.*

▶ **Hernando de Soto** *This Spanish explorer was one of the early explorers of the American West. He discovered the Missouri River in 1541.*

◀ **Mineral: *Diamonds*** *Arkansas is the only diamond-producing state. This fact is reflected in the diamond shape on the state flag.*

Michigan

The Wolverine State

Motto:

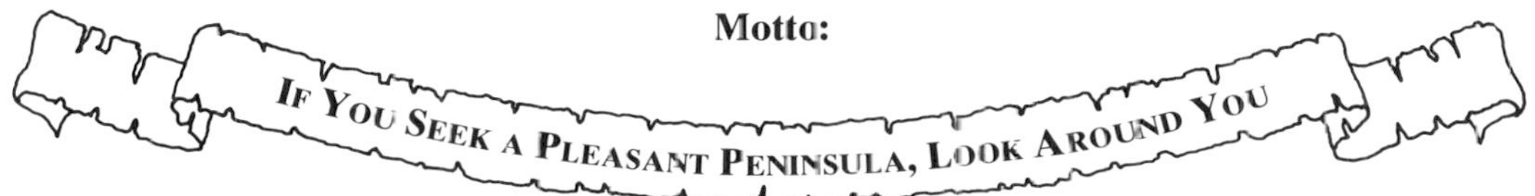

On January 26 1837, Michigan became the 26th state. The territory was first explored by Etienne Brulé in 1622 and the French settled at Sault St. Marie in 1668. After the Treaty of Paris, the British gained control. The United States took over in 1796, and Michigan was organized as a separate Territory in 1805. To its Native Americans, Michigan was the original "Happy Hunting Ground," its forests alive with game. After the Erie Canal opened in 1825, white settlers streamed in, taking over the land.

The influx of settlers resulted in great damage to the countryside. Whole forests were cut down and some animal species such as the wild turkey, the passenger pigeon, and the grayling trout disappeared. In 1920, Michigan introduced a conservation program, and today visitors can enjoy beautiful unspoilt scenery. Tourism is now the state's second largest industry. Michigan is famed for its automobiles and also manufactures furniture, machinery, iron and steel, chemicals, and breakfast foods. It also has large mineral deposits and is an important agricultural state.

▲ **State flag:** *The state coat of arms contains the word* TUEBOR, *"I shall defend."*

▶ **The Great Lakes**
The Great Lakes are a haven for wildlife, including many birds such as quail, ducks, and trumpeter swans.

▼ **Detroit**
Say "Detroit" and you say "automobiles." More cars are made here than in any other city in the world.

▲ **Fish:** ***Trout and brook trout***
These freshwater fish are popular food and game fish. They are found in many rivers and streams.

▶ **Canal transport**
The canals of Sault St. Marie are an important part of the water-transport network based on the Great Lakes.

Florida

The Sunshine State

On March 3 1845, Florida became the 27th state to join the Union. Originally settled by the Spanish, Florida contains the oldest buildings in the United States. Fort St. Augustine was built in 1565, more than 50 years after the Spanish explorer Ponce de León visited the area. Sir Francis Drake, a famous English naval captain, led a British attack in 1586. Britain finally gained full control of the area in 1763. During the Revolution, Florida remained loyal to Britain, but after the Treaty of Paris in 1783 it reverted to Spain. The United States gained possession in 1819. During the Civil War it was a Southern stronghold, though some parts remained in Union hands.

Since then Florida has become an important agricultural state with citrus, beef, and lumber as the main products. There are also "high-tech" aerospace industries. Tourism contributes greatly to Florida's economy, with attractions as diverse as the Everglades National Park, the Florida Keys, and Disney World.

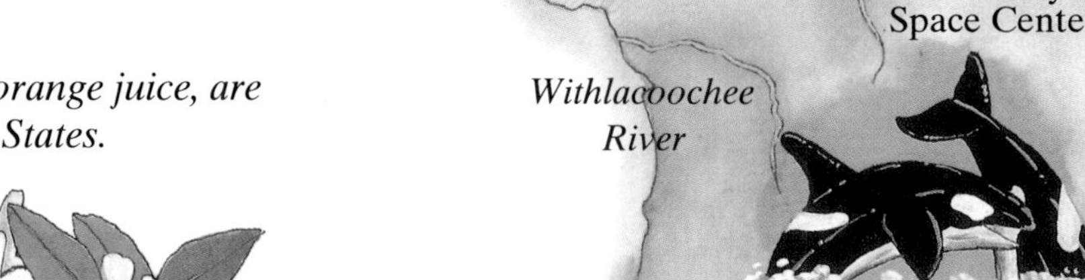

▶ **Flower:**
Orange blossom
Florida's oranges, and Florida orange juice, are famous throughout the United States.

▼ **State flag:**
The red saltire on a white field is said to reflect the Confederate battle flag. In the center is the State Seal.

◀ **The Everglades**
The Everglades are a unique wetland wilderness. The Seminole who lived there were the last Native Americans ever to sign a treaty with the United States.

▶ **The Space Flight Launch Center**
Cape Canaveral/Cape Kennedy is the center of the American Space Program.

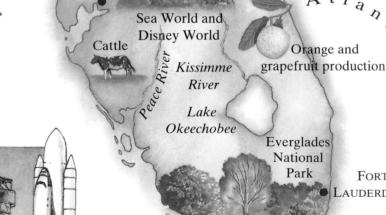

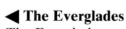

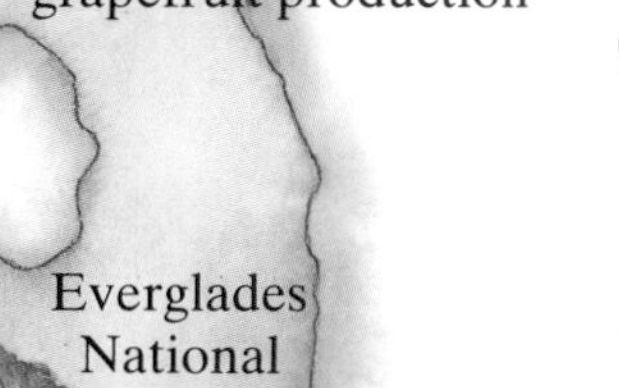

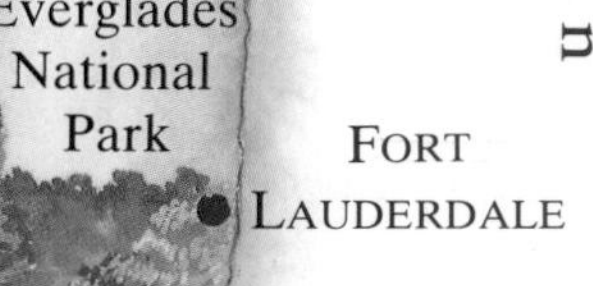

28

Texas

The Lone Star State

The 28th state of the Union, Texas joined on December 29 1845. The Spanish surveyed the coast in 1519, but the first Spanish settlement was not until 1682, at Ysleta. The French also settled here in 1685 and 1714, and by 1830 there were about 8,000 European settlers. The Spanish colony, later a part of independent Mexico, was open to settlement by Anglo-Americans, provided they took Mexican citizenship. Some settlers rebelled and set up the state of Texas (1836–1845). In 1860 they joined the Confederacy.

Cattle-raising was the original source of Texan wealth until oil was discovered in 1866. Texas is now the major producer of oil and natural gas. With its deserts, forests, mountains, plains and rivers, the state of Texas is larger than many countries. It is a major agricultural region and has more farmed land than any other part of the Union. Texas is also a thriving industrial and financial center with a strong cultural background.

▼ State flag:
The "Lone Star" originally flew over the Republic of Texas, after it broke away from Mexico and before it joined the USA.

▼ Seashell: ***Lightning whelk***
Whelks are sea-snails which prey on clams and other mollusks.

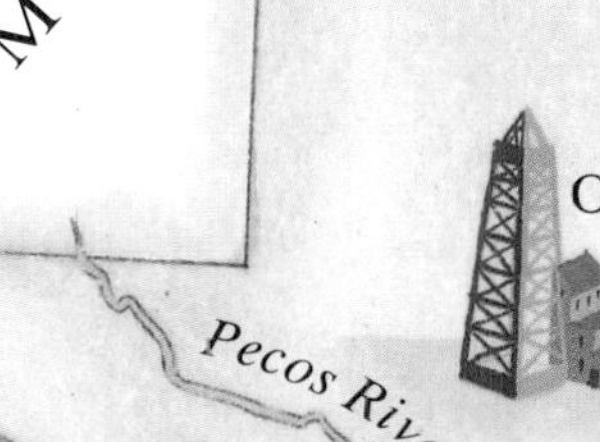

◀ Flower:
Bluebonnet
This relation of the lupin grows throughout the state.

▶ The Alamo
In 1836, fewer than 200 Texans defended the Alamo fort against General Santa Anna's 4,000-strong Mexican army. All the Texans, including Davy Crockett and Jim Bowie, were killed in the battle.

Davy Crockett

▶ Tree: ***Pecan***
The pecan is actually a large hickory nut; the name comes from the Algonquian or Cree pacan. *The pecan can grow up to 100 feet tall and bears distinctive bright pink nuts.*

29

Iowa

The Hawkeye State

Motto:

Our Liberties We Prize and Our Rights We Will Maintain

Iowa joined the Union on December 28 1846 as the 29th state, after an early complicated history. At various times it was ruled by France (after 1682 and from 1800 to 1803) and Spain (1762–1800). The area was included in the Louisiana Purchase of 1803. Settlers rapidly moved in to the region after more land was purchased from the local Native Americans. The Territory of Iowa was finally established in 1838 and in 1846, the present state was created.

An agricultural prairie state watered by the Mississippi and Missouri Rivers, Iowa used to be a patchwork of large and small farms. Today, more and more small farms are disappearing and most of the people live in small towns. There are few large urban areas. Des Moines, the capital, is one of the few big manufacturing centers. Service industries such as insurance and banking are also important. Although manufacturing and trade now earn a higher revenue than farming, pig and cattle farming are still important. Major crops include corn, oats, and soybeans.

▼ **State flag:**
The red, white, and blue colors commemorate the French rulers of Iowa.

▼ **Flower: *Wild rose***
The small but beautiful "rambling rose" grows throughout the state.

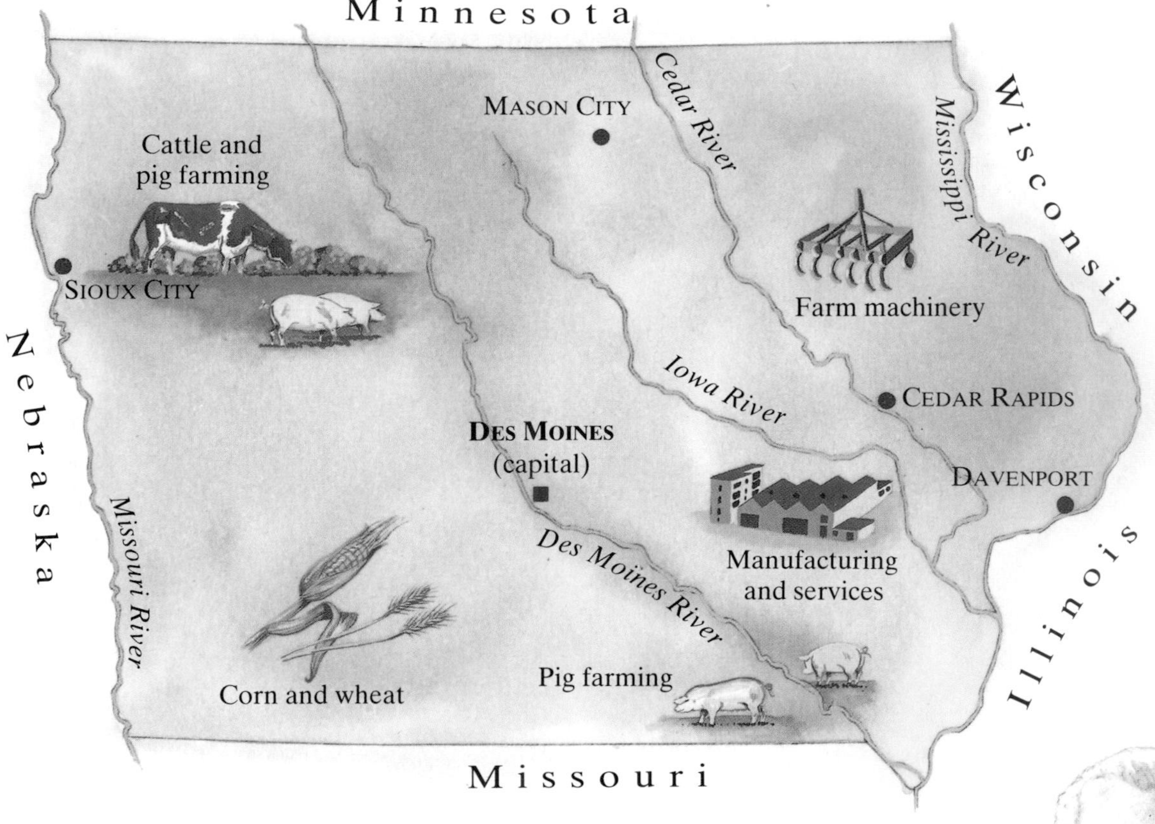

▶ **Buffalo Bill**
William Frederick Cody, better known as Buffalo Bill, is one of the most famous sons of Iowa. He was born in Scott County in 1846.

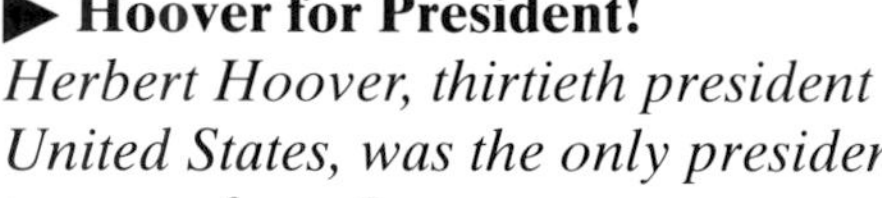

▶ **Hoover for President!**
Herbert Hoover, thirtieth president of the United States, was the only president ever to come from Iowa.

▶ **Bird: *Eastern goldfinch***
In the summer, the male bird develops beautiful golden plumage.

Wisconsin

The Badger State

Wisconsin became the 30th state, on May 29 1848. The first explorers and settlers were French, followed by a brief period of British rule. The United States finally took over in 1783. White settlement increased rapidly in the 1820s, leading to its organization as a separate Territory (1836). The local Native Americans were moved to separate "reservations." Statehood soon followed.

Wisconsin is mostly famous for dairy products, producing almost half the country's cheese, one-fifth of its butter, and one-sixth of its milk. Manufacturing is also important and the industrial belt in the southeast produces metal goods, machinery, and electrical components. There are also large mineral resources. The scenery is pretty rather than impressive, but it is great fishing country. Wisconsin's miles of waterways attract many tourists as well as being important commercial routes.

▼ **State Domestic Animal:** ***Dairy cow***
Wisconsin is "America's Dairy State."

▼ **Fish:** ***Muskellunge*** *This fighting fish, a variety of pike, is popular with anglers.*

▼ **Bird:** ***Mourning dove***
One of the most widespread pigeons, the mourning dove breeds throughout the United States. Its "cooing" song is familiar both in town and country.

▼ **State flag:**
The word "Wisconsin" and the date of joining the union were added to the state coat of arms on the flag in 1981.

▶ **Fossil:** ***Trilobite***
This extinct marine arthropod lived 500–200 million years ago. Many trilobites burrowed in sand or mud, scavenging or feeding on other small animals.

California

The Golden State

Motto:

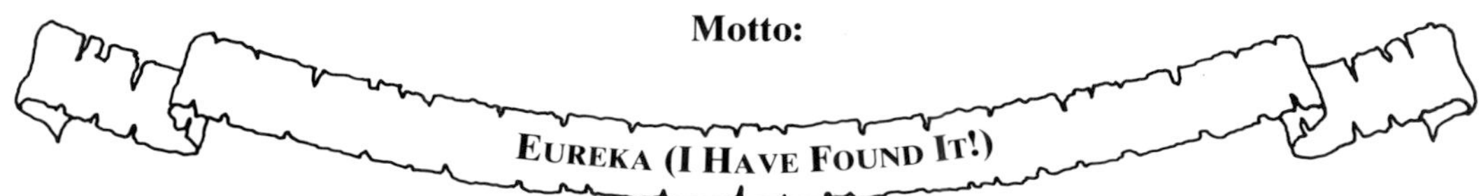

California was the 31st state to join the Union, on September 9 1850. The area was originally made up of "upper" or "Alta" California and "lower" or "Baja" California. In the 1530s, people believed "the Californias" were islands!

California was first colonized in the mid-1700s by the Spanish, who established many missions. Although Californians remained loyal to Spain during the Mexican Revolution, the area became part of Mexico in 1821. Many American settlers who had moved into Alta California wanted independence. After a few minor battles, the United States took over the area. Early in 1848, gold was discovered and by 1849 thousands of prospectors had traveled to California.

After the Gold Rush, agriculture became the most important industry. Today, California's farms produce more food than any other state. Oil, high-technology industries, banking, and entertainment have also helped to make it the wealthiest state, and its striking scenery, mild climate, and exciting cities are a tourist's paradise.

▼ **State flag:**
The flag depicts the state animal, the grizzly bear.

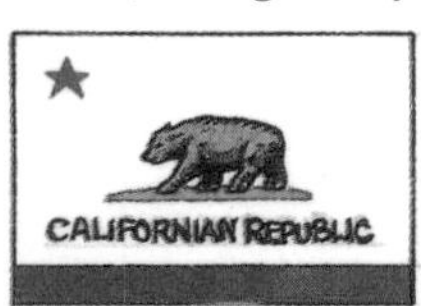

▼ **Animal:** ***Grizzly bear***
Now almost extinct, the grizzly bear is protected in national parks and zoos. Large adults can grow up to 7 feet long and weigh 900 lbs.

▲ **Tree:** ***Californian redwood***
The tallest living trees, redwoods are often over 300 feet high. They grow in the coastal fog belt from southwestern Oregon to central California.

▼ **Fish:** ***Golden trout***
The golden trout is found in clear mountain streams throughout the western states. It weighs up to 6 lbs and has a dark spotted body with a red stripe along the belly.

▼ **Bird:** ***Valley quail***
The Californian, or valley, quail has a distinctive plume of feathers that curls forward over its head.

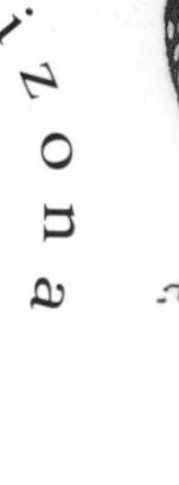

▶ **Flower:**
Californian poppy
The large four-petaled flowers only open in the sunlight. They range in color from deep orange to pale cream, and grow wild throughout the state.

Minnesota

The Gopher State

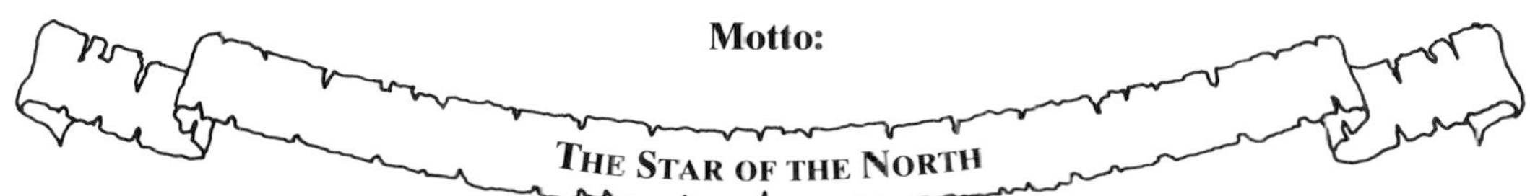

The 32nd state, Minnesota joined the Union on May 11 1858. The land is mostly flat, from the movement of glaciers across it 10,000 years ago, with very rich soil. A major dairy state, many crops including corn, wheat, oats, flax, and soybeans are also grown. Minnesota is sometimes called "the Bread and Butter State."

The first settlers were the French in the late 1600s. Part of the Louisiana Purchase, the area was not colonized until 1819 when the first American settlement was founded. Immigration was slow until lumbermen came to exploit the forests. The western part of the state was opened to settlement in 1851, and many people came from Norway and Sweden in the 1880s and 1890s. A considerable Scandinavian influence remains to this day.

Minnesota's largest industries are agriculture and food processing. Iron mining, and pulp and paper manufacture are also important. The state is dominated by Minneapolis—St. Paul, the "Twin Cities," an important cultural center where nearly half of Minnesotans live.

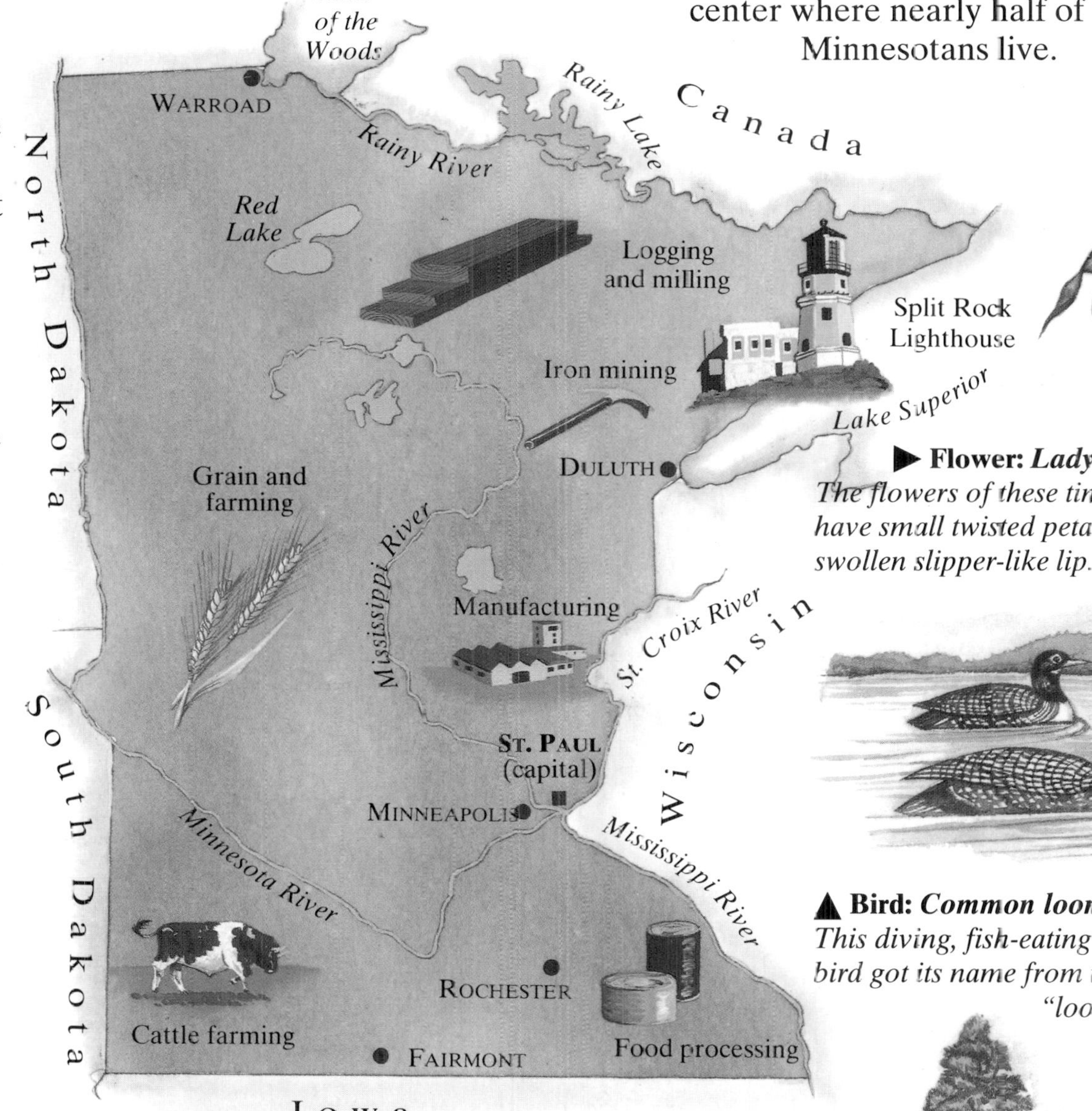

▼ **State flag:**
The state seal shows a white settler watching a displaced Native American riding westwards.

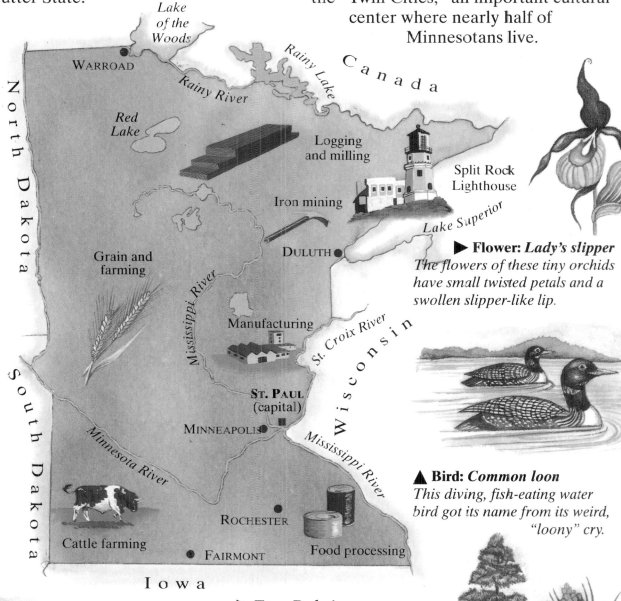

▼ **"10,000 Lakes"**
Known as the "land of 10,000 lakes," Minnesota has many tiny lakes in the Superior Highlands. The largest is the Lake of the Woods.

▶ **Flower: *Lady's slipper***
The flowers of these tiny orchids have small twisted petals and a swollen slipper-like lip.

▲ **Bird: *Common loon***
This diving, fish-eating water bird got its name from its weird, "loony" cry.

▶ **Tree: *Red pine***
This tall, stately tree, also known as the Norway pine, can grow up to 90 feet. It produces dark, heavy, close-grained wood.

33

Oregon

The Beaver State

Motto:

Oregon was the 33rd state to join the Union, on February 14 1859. Spanish explorers may have glimpsed the state in 1543, and the English sailor Francis Drake probably sailed past the coast in 1579. For many years it was open to both British and American pioneers. Settlers arrived steadily after about 1818. In the 1840s, thousands of people came from the Midwest along the Oregon Trail. In 1846 the 49th parallel was established as the border with Canada.

Oregon has a strong tradition of farming and forestry. Apples and other fruit and vegetables are grown west of the Cascade Mountains. On the eastern side there are cattle and sheep as well as wheat. Timber and lumber remain the main industries. Oregon is the nation's leading timber state, almost half the land is forested. The Columbia River System provides hydroelectric power, water for farming and industry, as well as shipping channels. Tourism is of increasing importance. Visitors are attracted not just by the rivers and the mountains, up to 11,245 feet high, but by such sights as Crater Lake, which at 1,932 feet is the deepest in the country.

▼ **State flag:**
On one side of the flag is a state shield surrounded by 33 stars and the date 1859. On the other is a beaver.

▼ **Flower: *Oregon grape***
The yellow-flowered Oregon grape has purple grape-like fruit in the fall.

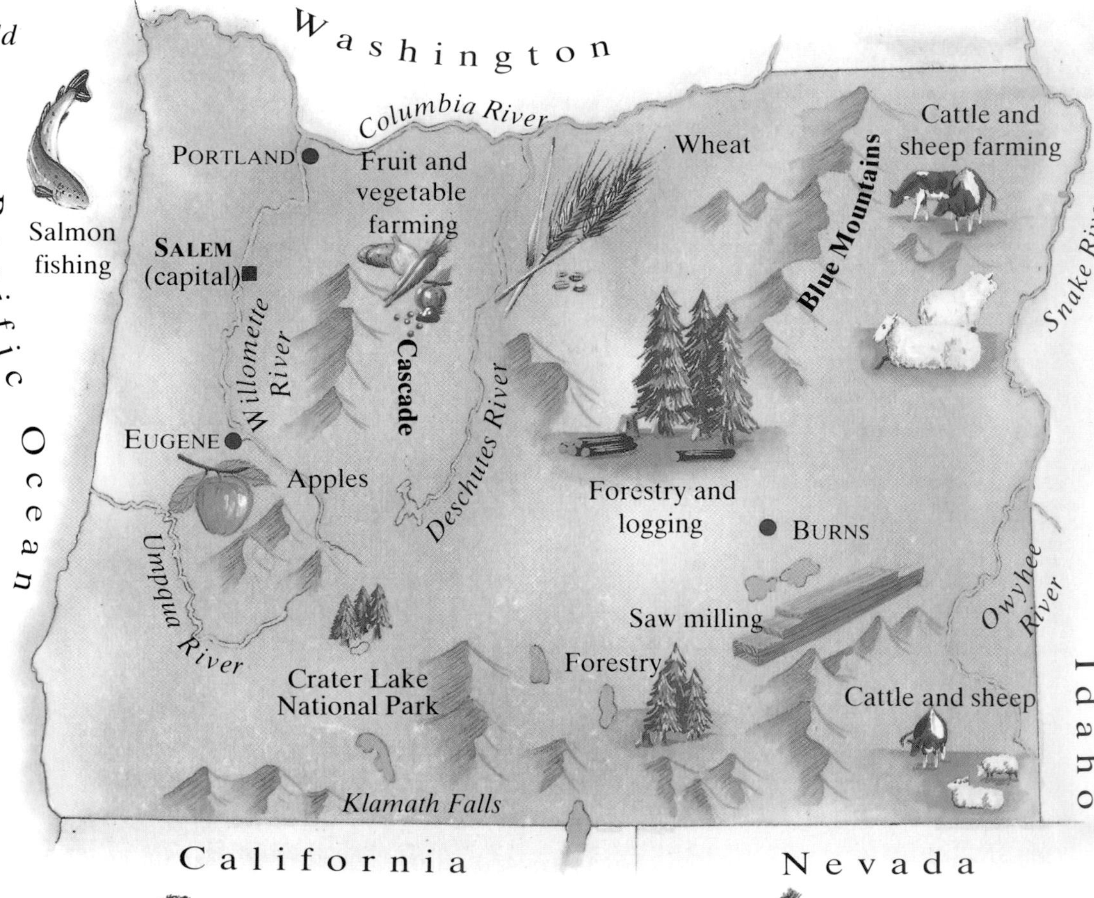

▶ **Rock: *Thunder-egg***
"Thunder-eggs" or geodes conceal a magical core of crystals within their ordinary looking shells.

▶ **Tree: *Douglas fir***
The mighty Douglas fir fills Oregon's vast forests, along with spruce, and western hemlock.

▶ **Animal: *Beaver***
This large aquatic rodent lives in family groups building a "lodge" of felled logs and mud.

Kansas

The Sunflower State

Motto:

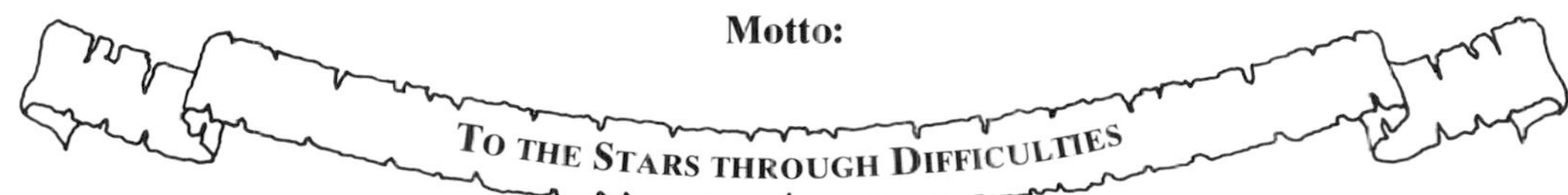

Kansas, the 34th state, joined the Union on January 29 1861. The region had been explored by Spaniards from Mexico in 1541, but until 1854 it was mainly settled by Indian tribes. Kansas was known as "the great American desert" because there were hardly any trees. The sandy soil was believed to be unsuitable for growing crops or raising cattle.

White settlement of the area increased rapidly after Kansas entered the Union, and by 1890 most of the land was occupied. Agriculture was the dominant industry and vast areas of the prairie were plowed up. In the 1930s, overfarming led to barren "dust-bowls" where the topsoil blew away.

Today manufacturing and industry are as important as agriculture. Kansas is the leading state for wheat and sorghum production; hay, beef, and pigs are also important. Wichita is a major center for aircraft manufacture. Food processing is also a major industry. There are large mineral resources including oil, gas, and coal.

▼ **State flag:**
The flag incorporates the state seal and the sunflower.

◀ **Bird: *Western meadowlark***
With its yellow breast marked with black, the meadowlark has a distinctive "bubbling" song.

▲ **Flower:**
Sunflower
Golden bright sunflowers grow everywhere in Kansas, even by the side of the road.

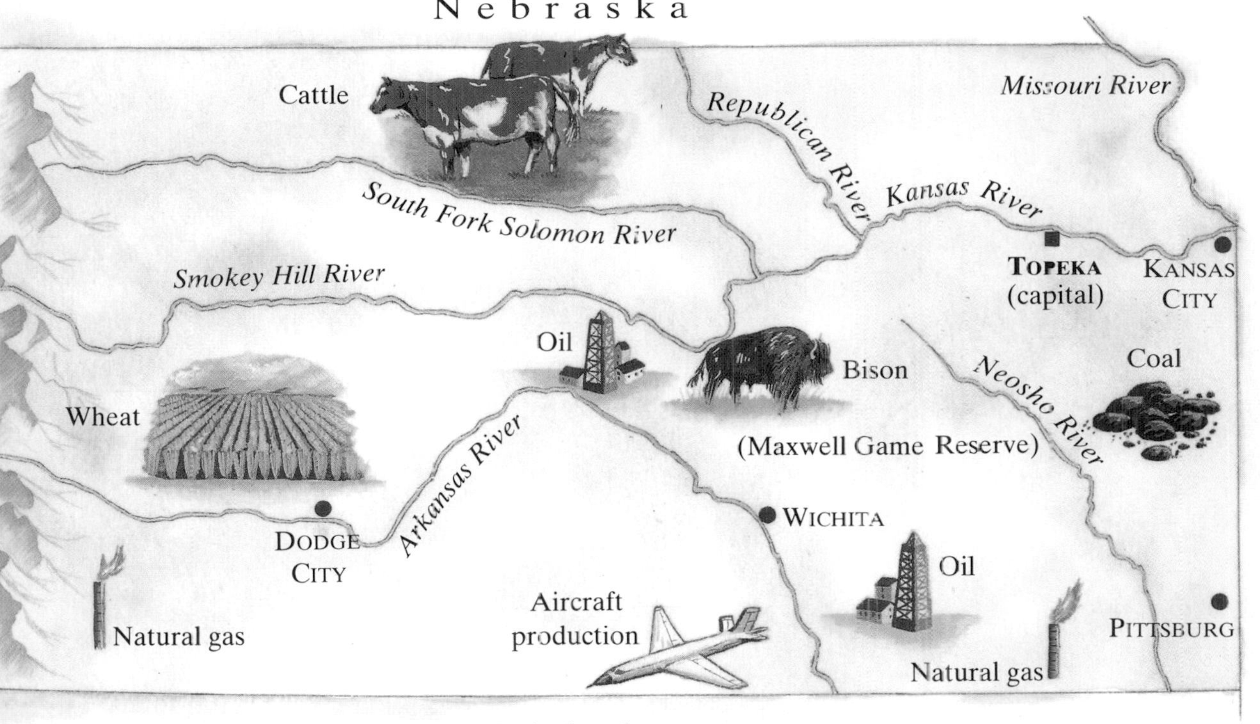

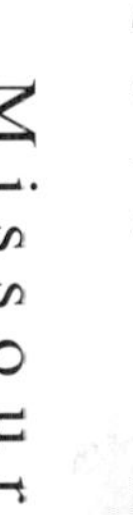

▶ **Animal: *Bison***
Huge herds of bison once roamed the Midwest. They were hunted almost to extinction, and are now found only on reserves.

▶ **"Amber waves of grain"**
"For purple mountains' majesty
And amber waves of grain" —
Kansas is the main wheat-growing area — the "amber waves" in the song "America."

West Virginia

The Mountain State

Motto:

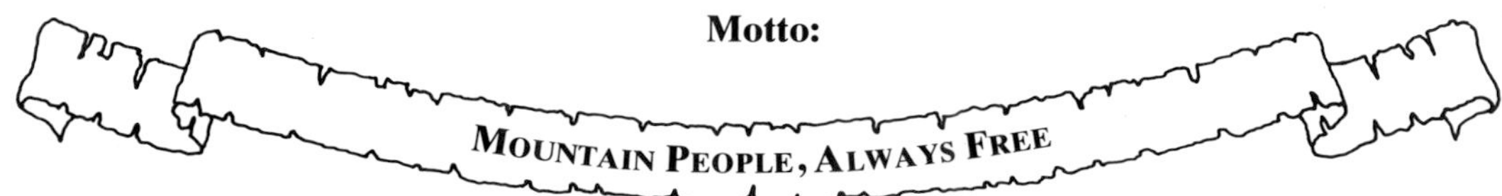

West Virginia joined the Union as the 35th state, on June 20 1863. The state was carved from Virginia, which had joined the Confederacy, because West Virginians wanted to stay with the Union.

West Virginia is a mountainous state that for most of its history has lived by farming, timber production, and coal mining. Some of the finest hardwood forests in the country are in West Virginia, though heavy logging has reduced them greatly. Since the 1970s, many conservation measures have been taken to protect the environment. Industrial cities in the Ohio and Monongahela valleys are dependent on local resources. Natural gas, oil, and coal are all produced in the state. Manufacturing of iron, steel, glass, and chemicals has also been growing in importance. There are many areas of extraordinary natural beauty, and increased tourism has added substantially to West Virginia's economy.

▼ State flag:
The state coat of arms shows a miner and a farmer beside a rock which bears the date of West Virginia's entry to the Union.

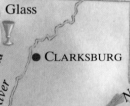

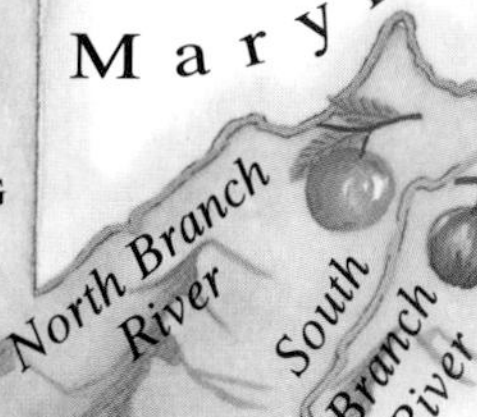

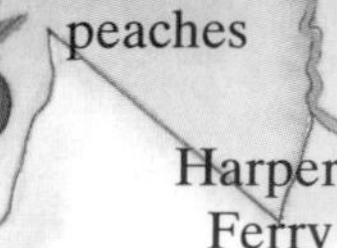

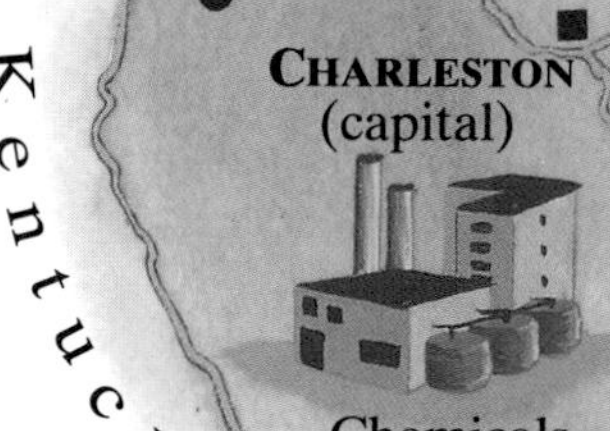

▲ Folk music
West Virginia is the greatest state of the Union for folk music, probably because of the musical traditions brought by Irish and Scottish settlers.

▲ John Brown
"John Brown's body lies a-moldering in the grave" — the anti-slavery campaigner was hanged for leading a raid on Harper's Ferry.

► Animal: *Black bear*
The American black bear can weigh up to 600 lbs. It climbs well and eats a variety of food including berries, pine cones, and small animals.

▲ Coal mining and timber
Two natural resources, coal and timber, form an important part of West Virginia's economy.

Nevada

The Silver State

Motto:

Nevada joined the Union as the 36th state, on October 31 1864. No European visited the state until 1775, when a Franciscan friar passed through on his way to California. The area became part of the United States after the Mexican War of 1848 and for two years remained a part of California. From 1850 to 1861 it belonged to Utah. In 1859, the discovery of the famous Comstock Lode, the world's richest silver deposits, led to colonization by prospectors and the formation of Nevada Territory in 1861.

Nevada has vast plateaus with mountain peaks rising to over 10,000 feet. An arid state, cattle and sheep are the main agricultural products. Industries include mining, copper smelting, stone, clay and glass products, food processing, and electronics. Today, over half the population and much of the industry is centered around Las Vegas and Reno.

▼ **State flag:**
The state seal is in the upper half, not the center, and the words "Battle Born" refer to when Nevada joined the Union.

▼ **Hoover Dam**
The Hoover Dam was built across the Colorado River in 1936. As well as providing water and hydroelectric power, it is a great tourist attraction.

▶ **Las Vegas**
Las Vegas is the gambling capital of the world, with millions of dollars a day risked on games of chance.

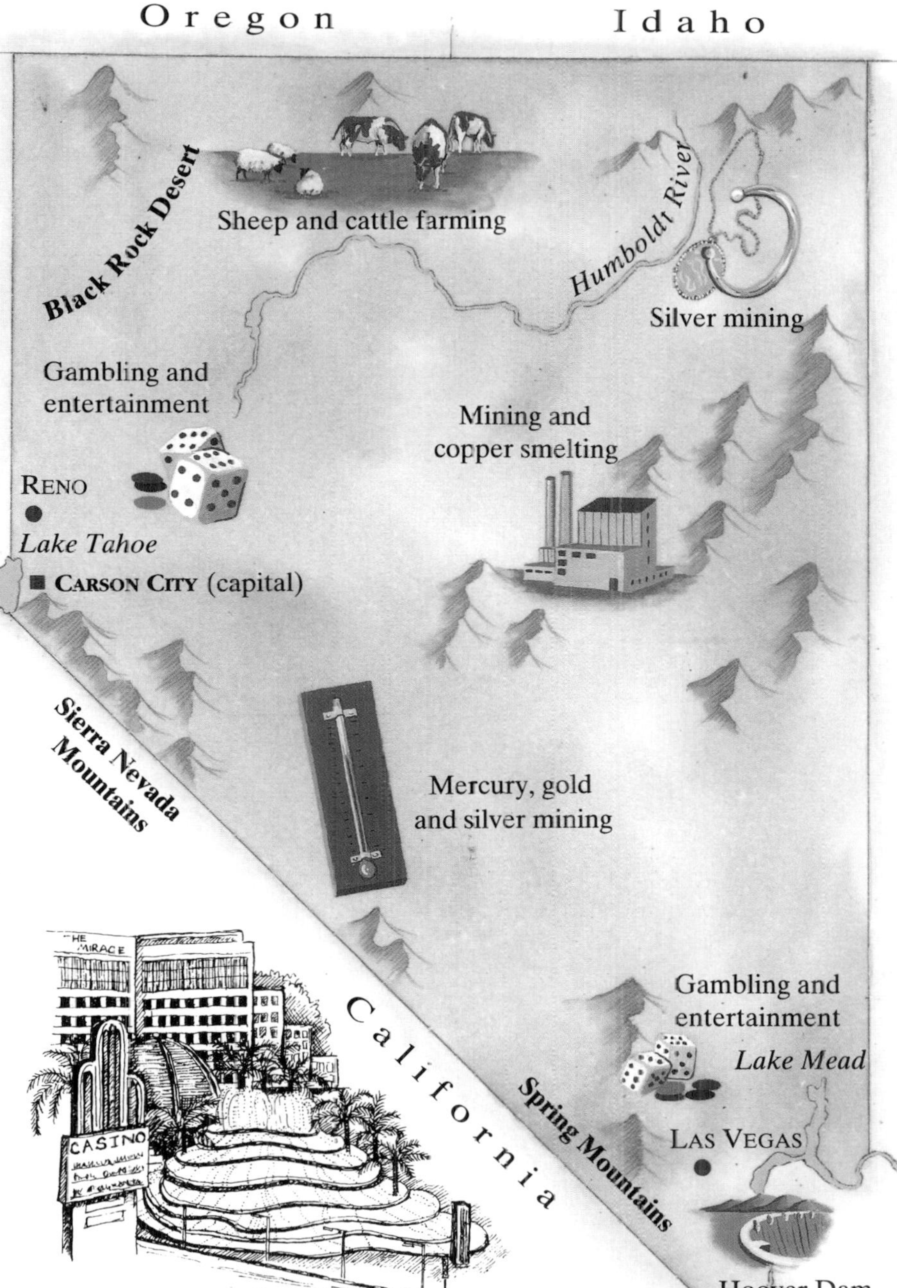

▲ **Tree: *Bristlecone pine***
Some bristlecone pines are thousands of years old, among the oldest living things on the planet.

▲ **Flower: *Sagebrush***
The smell of the sagebrush at dusk, and its purple-blue foliage, are an unforgettable part of Nevada.

Nebraska

The Cornhusker State

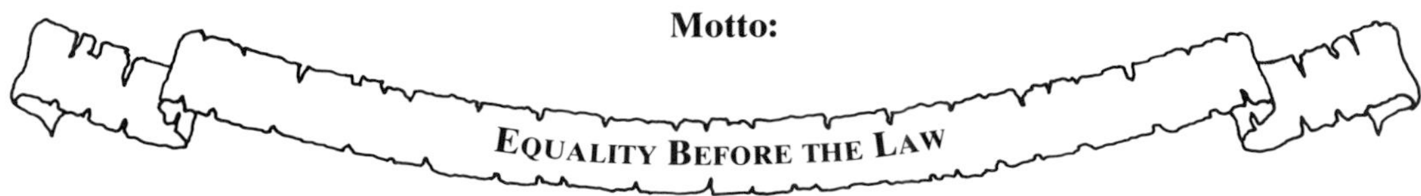

Nebraska became the 37th state on March 1 1867. Acquired by the United States as a part of the Louisiana Purchase in 1803, it was explored and occasionally exploited for furs by the Spanish and French. The British also claimed it but the Treaty of Paris in 1763 recognized Spanish rights. The earliest permanent European settlement was in 1823. Treaties with the Native Americans ceded their lands to the United States and settlement extended westwards.

Nebraska became, and remains, a leading producer of corn, wheat, and livestock. The land is mostly rolling plains, with hills in the north and east. In places the rich, fertile soil is 200 feet deep. The main manufacturing industries have always been food processing and similar trades. Oil was discovered in 1939, and Nebraska also produces natural gas. The population of this enormous area, the 16th largest state, is very small, under two million. Most people live in the industrial east, leaving much of the state lightly populated.

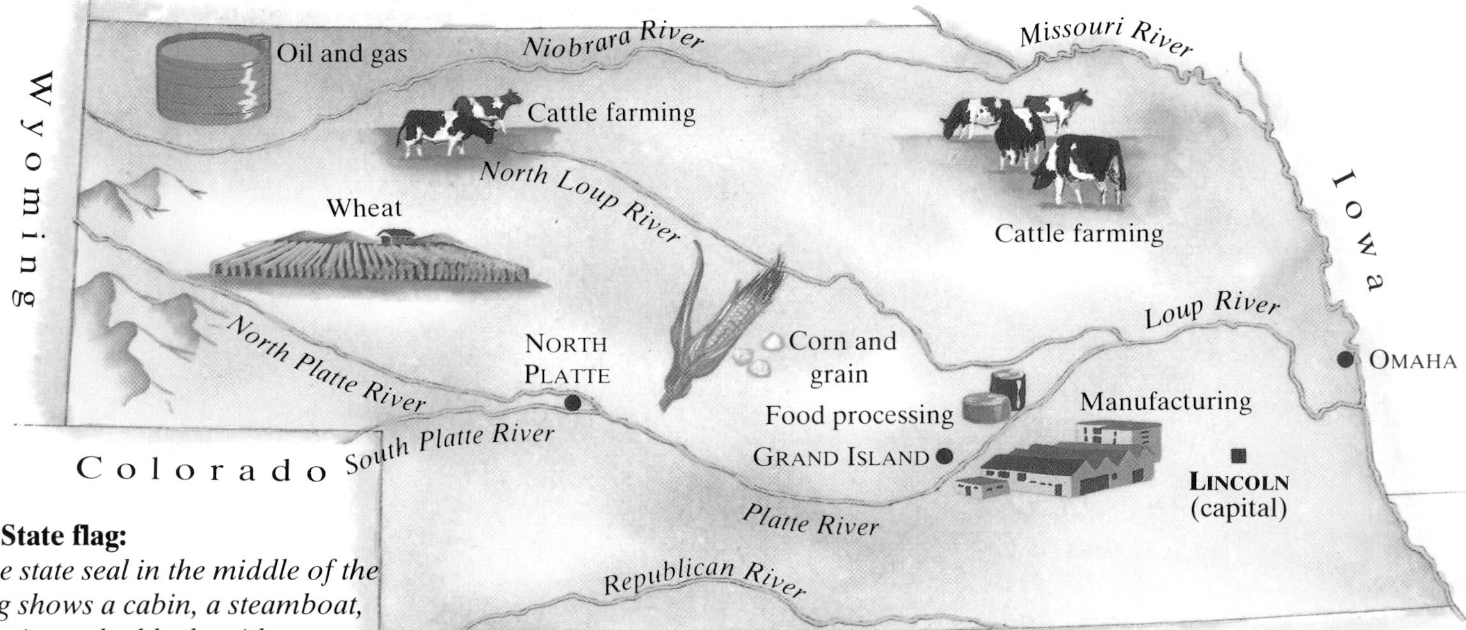

▼ **State flag:**
The state seal in the middle of the flag shows a cabin, a steamboat, a train, and a blacksmith.

▶ **Tree: *Cottonwood***
This 90-foot North American poplar has seeds with cottony threads, making them look like a cotton boll.

◀ **Fossil: *Shaggy mammoth***
The huge, shaggy mammoth is the official state fossil of Nebraska.

▶ **Lewis and Clark**
Meriwether Lewis and William Clark went up the Missouri, across the Rockies, and then down the Columbian River to the Pacific. They explored the Yellowstone River on the return trip. The expedition established the United States claim to the Louisiana Purchase.

38

Colorado

Centennial State

Motto:

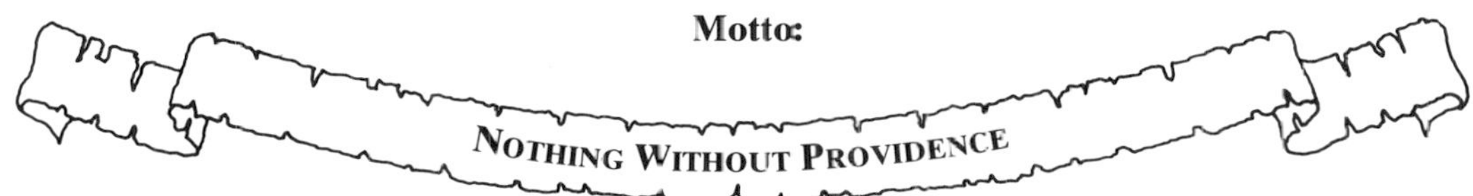

The name "Centennial State" marks the fact that Colorado joined the Union as its 38th state in the country's hundredth year: August 1 1876. Like many other southwestern states, Colorado was first explored by the Spanish in 1540. It was acquired by the United States as part of the Louisiana Purchase.

The Gold Rush of 1859 encouraged settlers to Colorado— 50,000 came in that year alone. Since then, many other metals have been discovered and mining continues to be important. Irrigation has turned what used to be semidesert into farmland. Corn, sugarbeet, and vegetables are produced as well as cattle, hogs, and sheep. Machinery, chemicals, military equipment, and food products are the major industries.

Colorado is the highest state in the Union and the Rocky Mountains form a dramatic "spine" down the center. The capital Denver is known as the "Mile High City." Winter sports have encouraged tourism.

▼ **State flag:**
The blue symbolizes the clear blue skies; the white, the snowy mountain peaks; and the yellow, with its "C" for "Colorado," the sun.

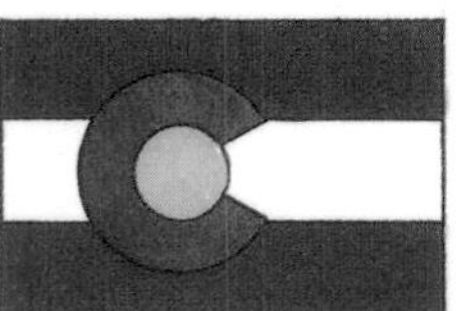

▶ **Tree: *Blue Mountain spruce***
The Engleman or Blue Mountain spruce has pale blue-green spines and long orange-brown cones.

▶ **Animal: *Rocky Mountain bighorn sheep***
The massive horns of the ram weigh as much as the rest of the animal's skeleton!

▲ **Gemstone: *Aquamarine***
This beautiful stone is from the same family as the emerald.

▲ **Flower:**
Rocky Mountain columbine
The columbine, a protected flower, also features in the state song "Where the Columbines Grow."

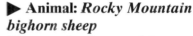

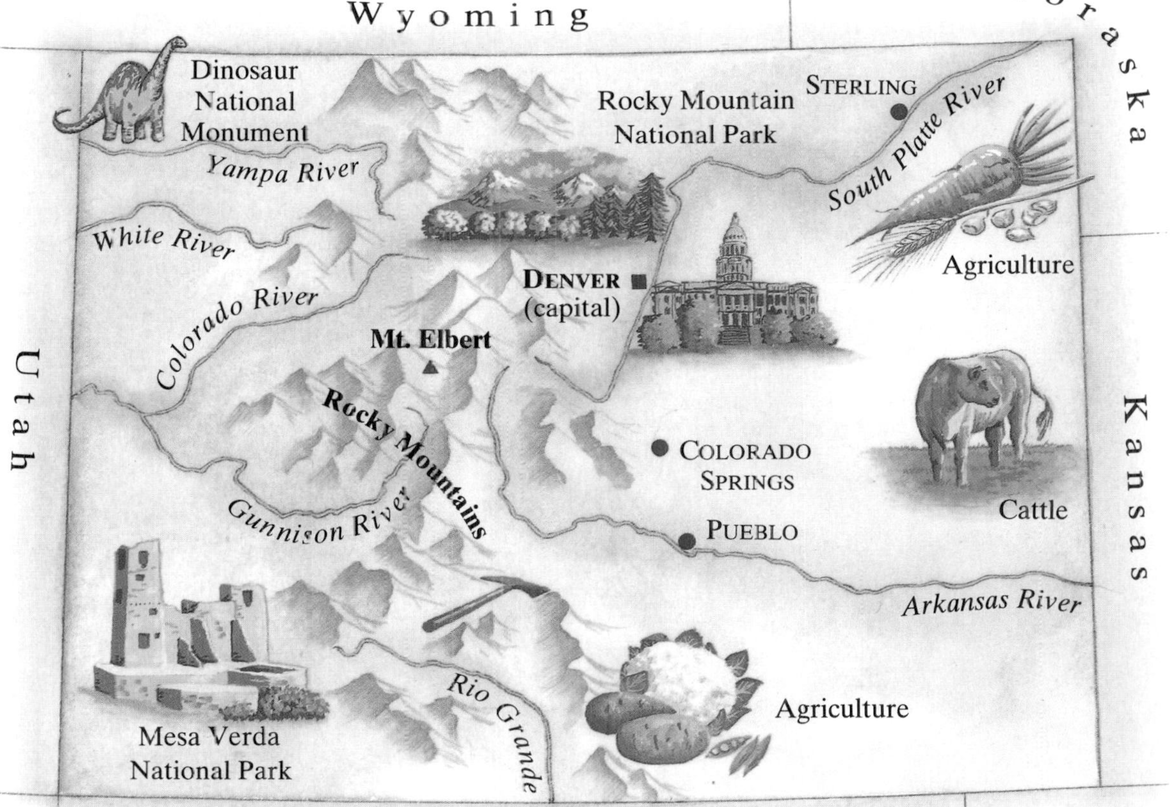

North Dakota

The Sioux State

Motto:

On November 2 1889, North Dakota became the 39th state. Roosevelt wrote about its "curious, fantastic beauty" in 1884, and this still holds true today. For many years after its first exploration by the French in the 1730s, the region was mainly the haunt of fur trappers and traders. The Sioux discouraged early settlers and hostilities grew when the US Army built forts along the rivers. White settlement increased rapidly in the 1870s.

The railroads and the Homestead Act further boosted white settlement, with many immigrants coming from Norway, Russia, and other northern European countries. Scandinavian and Native American folk traditions play an important role in the state's culture. North Dakota still has a small population: well under a million in the early 1990s. Most of the state's economy centers on agriculture: wheat, rye, oats, and barley grown on large farms. Coal and oil reserves, among the country's largest, are also being exploited.

Canada
Montana
Minnesota
South Dakota
Oil
Souris River
Minot
Lake Sakakawea
Garrison Reservoir
Devil's Lake
Barley
Grand Forks
Red River
Missouri River
Coal
Rye
James River
Cheyenne River
Bismarck (capital)
Fargo
Wheat
Cattle farming
Missouri River
Ellendale
Oats

▼ **State flag:**
The flag incorporates the regimental colors of the 1st North Dakota Infantry in the Spanish–American war.

▼ **Sacajawea**
The Lewis and Clark Expedition in 1805 explored the Louisiana Purchase and the surrounding area with the help of Sacajawea ("Bird Woman").

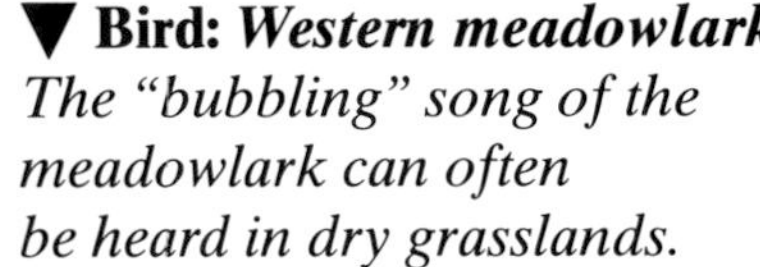

▼ **Bird: *Western meadowlark***
The "bubbling" song of the meadowlark can often be heard in dry grasslands.

◀ **Sioux**
The Sioux were originally a relatively peaceful plains tribe whose lives were transformed by the introduction of the horse.

▶ **Scottish Highlanders**
The first serious settlers, in 1819, were Lord Selkirk's Highlanders from Scotland.

South Dakota

The Coyote State

Motto:

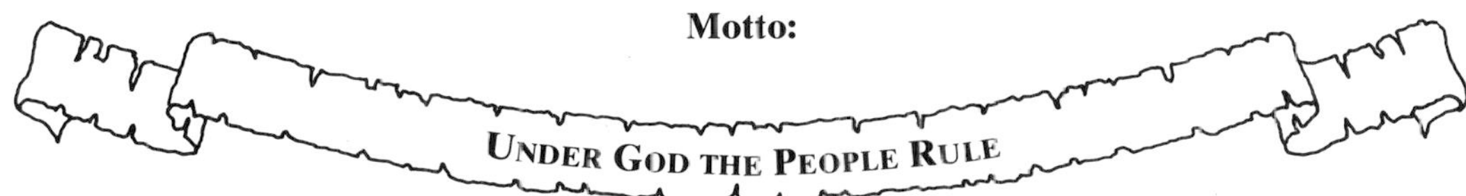

South Dakota became the 40th state on November 2 1889. The area was not explored by Europeans until 1742, and was occupied by both France and Spain at various times. Part of the Louisiana Purchase of 1803, the first real settlements came in the late 1850s and 1860s. The discovery of gold in the Black Hills attracted many settlers. Agreements with the Native Americans opened up the state to homesteaders and settlement increased rapidly. The local tribes were restricted to designated reservations.

Today there are still fewer than three-quarters of a million people living here. Livestock and livestock products are the mainstay of the economy. Although South Dakota has one of the largest gold mines, other mining is minimal. Major industries include food products, machinery, and wood products. The scenery is often spectacular, with mountain peaks climbing to 7,240 feet, impressive caves, rock needles and buttes, and many lakes, rivers, and gorges. Countless fossils have been found, including dinosaurs from 40 million years ago.

▶ **State flag:**
The state seal now appears on both sides of the flag: on the original 1909 version, the two sides were different.

◀ **Flower:** ***American pasqueflower***
This anemone blooms around Easter, which is why it is also called the paschal flower.

▲ **Animal:** ***Coyote***
This name for the prairie wolf entered the language via Spanish from the Native American Nahuatl tongue.

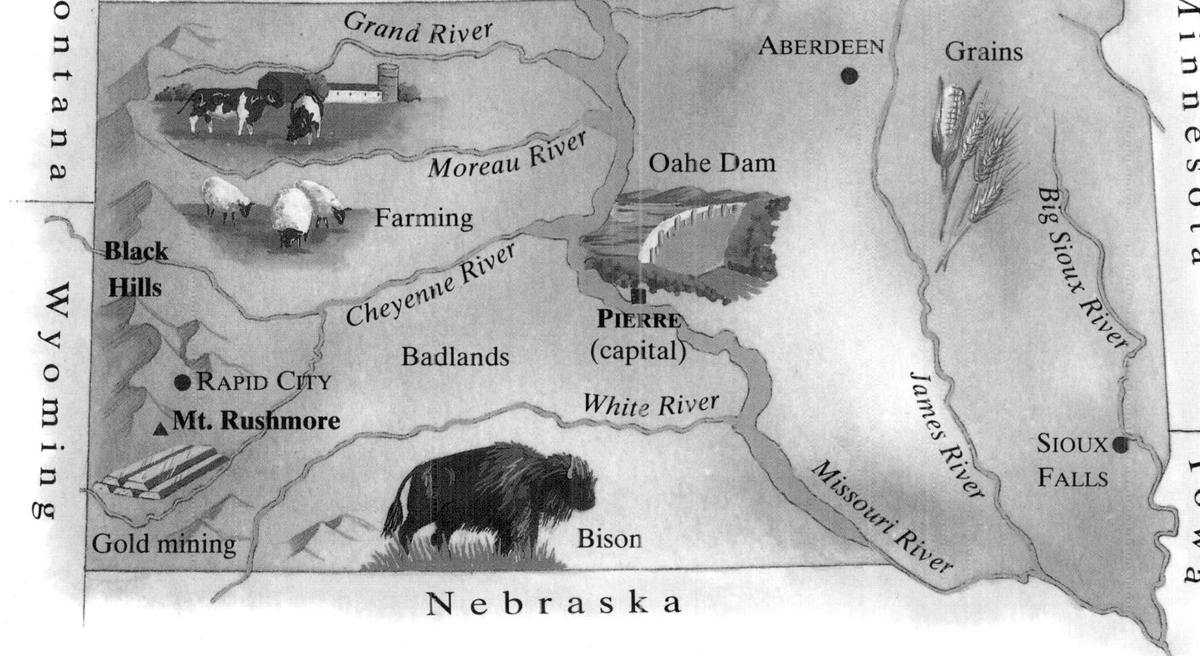

▼ **Wounded Knee**
The Native American Ghost Dancing movement ended when over 200 Sioux were killed at Wounded Knee in 1890. There are many Native American reservations in South Dakota.

◀ **President rock**
Mount Rushmore, with its enormous carved heads of Washington, Jefferson, Lincoln, and Roosevelt, is probably the best-known landmark in South Dakota.

41

Montana

The Treasure State

Motto:

Montana was admitted as the 41st state, on November 8 1889. It is huge — the fourth largest state — and thinly populated, with fewer than a million people in the early 1990s. The Rockies cross the state from northwest to southeast, and there are many lesser local ranges. The rest of the state is flat, typical Great Plains country. The first settlement was not until 1807, two years after the Lewis and Clark Expedition which explored so much of the West. Serious immigration started only when gold was discovered in 1858. There were many more strikes after that, and in the 1870s silver was also found. Mining, especially of copper, is still important today.

Montana's economy is mostly agricultural, cattle and wheat farming being of greatest importance. Cattle and sheep raising in Montana began when the first cattle herd was driven overland from Texas in 1866. The native bison, however, were almost wiped out in the 1870s and 1880s. Other crops include barley and sugarbeet. Forestry products, pulp, and paper are vital to western Montana.

▶ **State flag:**
The flag with its view of the Great Falls of the Missouri River dates back to 1905.

◀ **Flower: *Bitterroot***
This plant's pale pink or white flowers form a rosette. The swollen root may be bitter, but it is nutritious and edible.

Canada
North Dakota
South Dakota
Idaho
Wyoming
Glacier National Park
Wheat
Milk River
Coal
Missouri River
Forestry and lumber
GREAT FALLS
Missouri River
Fort Peck Reservation
MISSOULA
Rocky Mountains
HELENA (capital)
Yellowstone River
BUTTE
Metal products
BILLINGS
Cattle
Mining
Oil
Crow Reservation
Powder River

▲ **Tree: *Ponderosa pine***
This huge pine can grow up to 200 feet tall and 8 feet in diameter.

◀ **Custer's Last Stand**
Custer made his Last Stand in Montana, when he misjudged the strength of opposing forces at Greasy Grass Creek, better known as Little Bighorn. There are now several Native American reservations in Montana, notably the Crow Reservation.

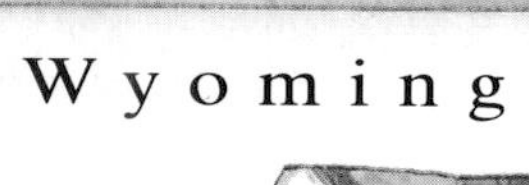

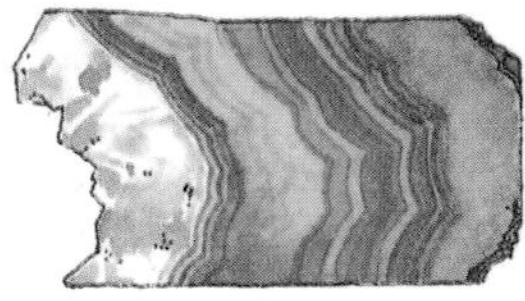

◀ **Minerals:**
Agate and sapphire
Both of these attractive semi-precious stones are found in the state.

Washington

The Evergreen State

Motto:

Washington became the 42nd state on November 11 1889. The land was not even sighted by a European until 1774. For many years fur traders were the main visitors to the area. From 1818 to 1846 the Oregon Territory was jointly administered by Britain and the United States. The British Hudson Bay Company dominated the area until the 1840s. In 1846, Oregon Territory became a part of the United States, and Washington separated from Oregon in 1853. The state was named after George Washington.

Gold was discovered in the 1850s, but gold mining itself did not bring great wealth to the state. Supplying the gold miners did: they needed food, tools, and lumber, and so trade and farming grew. Today, Washington remains a major wood-producing state, with wheat, fruit (especially apples), and cattle and dairy farming in the east. The leading industries are aircraft production and the generation of hydroelectricity. Washington's amazing and diverse scenery, including mountains, glaciers, forests, and lakes, is a great tourist attraction.

▶ **Flower: *Rhododendron***
Masses of rhododendrons grow in the wild throughout the state forming vistas of blazing color.

Canada
Pacific Ocean
Forestry
Okanogan River
Cattle farming
Manufacturing
Columbia River
Idaho
Olympic National Park
SEATTLE
SPOKANE
TACOMA
Water power
OLYMPIA (capital)
Mt. Rainier
Fruit farming
Fishing
Cascade Range
Snake River
Columbia River
Wheat
Forestry and paper making
Oregon

▼ **State flag:**
Washington is the only state to have its state seal (1881) alone on a green background.

▼ **Temperate rain forests**
Washington has one of the world's few temperate rain forests with 140 inches of rain a year.

◀ **Bird: *Willow goldfinch***
Goldfinches are seed-eating birds; the male's summer plumage is yellow with a black tail.

▶ **Boeing**
Boeing, probably the most important commercial aircraft company in the world, has its headquarters in Seattle.

Idaho

The Panhandle State

Motto:

Idaho became the 43rd state, on July 3 1890. The name comes from the Shoshone *Ee dah how*, "Where the sun comes down the mountain." Local tribes had lived in the area for at least 10,000 years before the territory was claimed by Spain, Russia, Great Britain, and the United States. Spain and Russia later dropped their claims to the area and in 1846, a British–American treaty gave the United States sole control of the land south of the 49th parallel.

Idaho now depends mainly on mining, cattle and sheep raising, and agriculture. There are silver, lead, zinc, tungsten, and even gold mines. Idaho is famous for its potatoes, though wheat, sugar beet, and other vegetables are also grown. The state has many natural wonders: the Shoshone Falls are 43 feet higher than Niagara; Mount Borah is 12,662 feet high; and Hells Canyon is the deepest gorge in the United States.

▼ **State flag:**
The state flag depicts the seal — a mountain landscape, supported by a miner and a woman with spear and scales — on a blue background.

▼ **Flower: *Syringa***
The syringa, or mock orange, has sweet-smelling cream-colored flowers that resemble orange blossom.

▼ **Bird: *Mountain bluebird***
The bright plumage of the bluebird flashes in the sun as it flies from shady tree to shady tree.

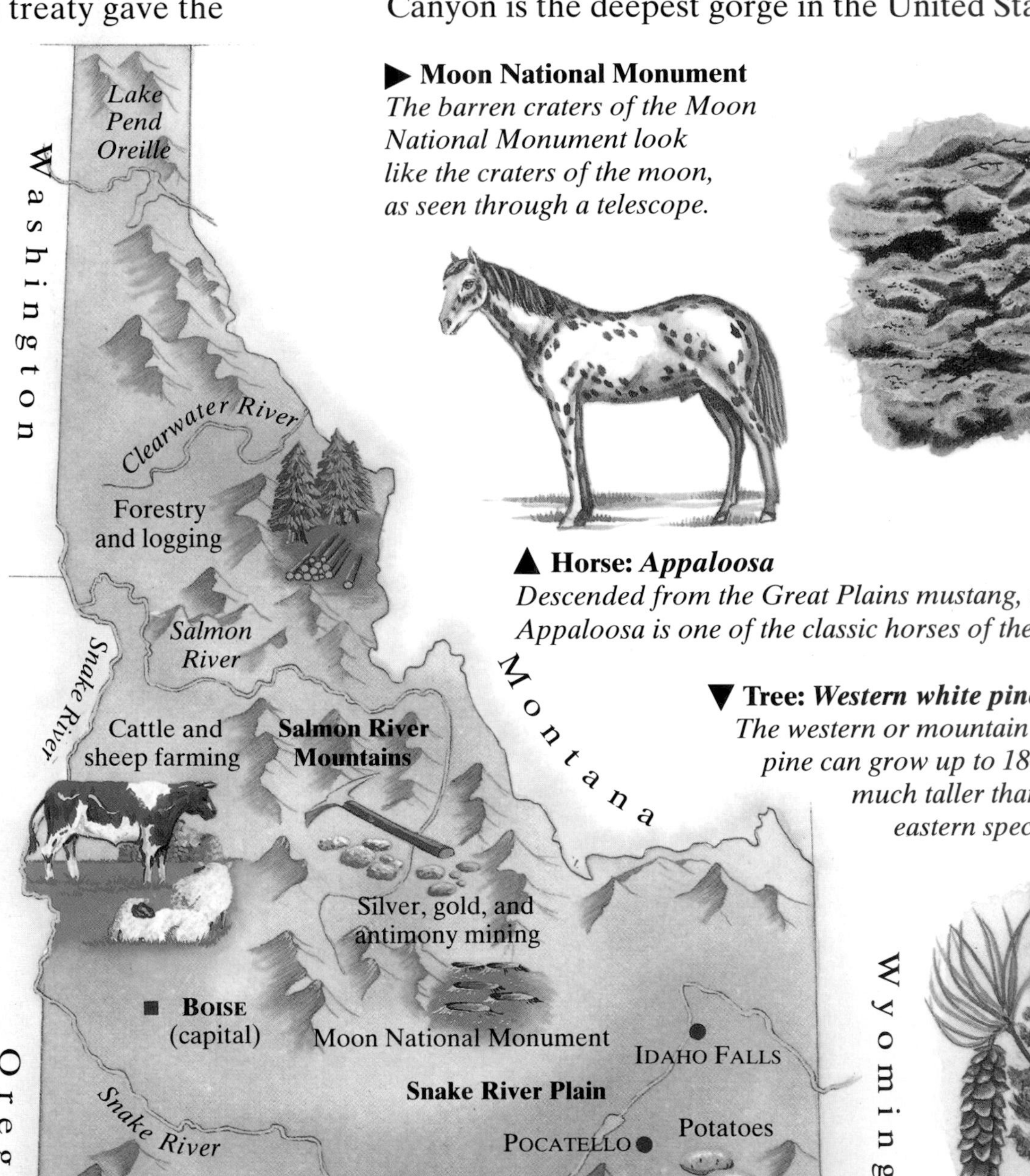

▶ **Moon National Monument**
The barren craters of the Moon National Monument look like the craters of the moon, as seen through a telescope.

▲ **Horse: *Appaloosa***
Descended from the Great Plains mustang, the Appaloosa is one of the classic horses of the West.

▼ **Tree: *Western white pine***
The western or mountain white pine can grow up to 180 feet, much taller than the eastern species.

Wyoming

The Equality State

Wyoming, admitted as the 44th state, on July 10 1890, was part of the territory bought in the Louisiana Purchase of 1803. Wars with Sioux and Shoshone tribes originally confined white settlement to the south. Later, US army campaigns opened up the north of the territory and the Native Americans were consigned to the Wind River Reservation. In the 1870s and 1880s herds of cattle were driven up from Texas to live off the rich grasses of the plains and white settlement expanded. In the mid-1880s, sheep-raising started to become important, giving rise to the "wars" between cattle and sheep men from 1890 to 1909.

Wyoming is "high plains" country, with central plains at 5,000 to 6,000 feet and mountain ranges with many peaks of over 13,000 feet. Today, most of Wyoming's wealth comes from sheep, cattle, and oil. There is very little manufacturing, but the area has many natural resources including oil, natural gas, coal, and uranium. Local attractions, such as the Yellowstone National Park with its hot springs, bring in many tourists.

▼ State flag:
The state seal appears on the outline of a buffalo, on a red-white-and-blue flag.

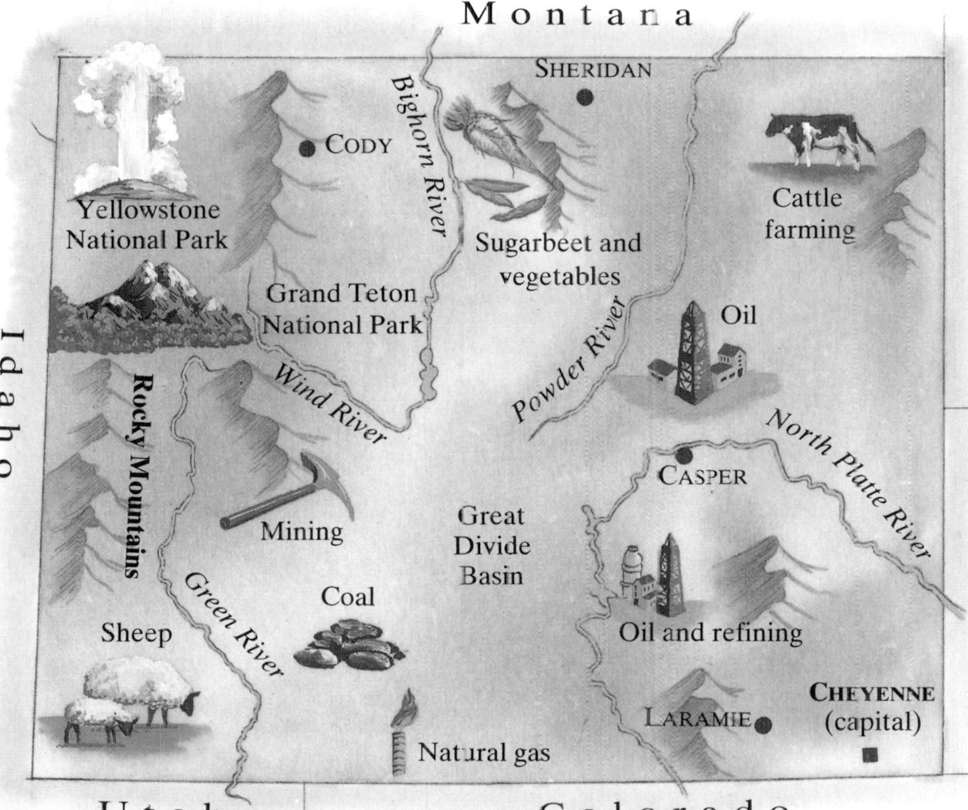

▲ "Votes for Women"
The nickname "The Equality State" came from the fact that Wyoming gave women the vote as early as 1869. It was the first state to do so.

▲ Flower: ***Indian paintbrush***
These bright distinctive flowers get their name from an Indian legend. A boy trying to paint a sunset threw down his brushes. The flowers grew where his brushes landed.

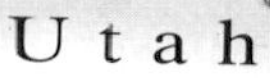

▶ Insignia: ***Bucking horse***
Cowboys and rodeos are central to Wyoming's image and its tourist attractions.

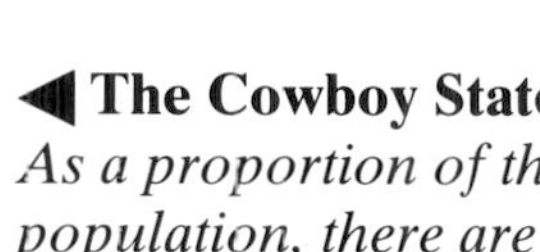

◀ The Cowboy State
As a proportion of the population, there are probably more real, working cowboys in Wyoming than anywhere else. Many small towns still retain the original "western buildings."

Utah

The Beehive State

Motto:

Utah joined the Union as the 45th state, on January 4 1896. The area was originally explored by the Spanish in 1776. Southeastern Utah was one of the last parts of the United States to be explored. The home of the Ute, from whom the state got its name, Utah has spectacular scenery: mountains almost 13,500 feet tall, incredible rock formations, including many natural bridges and fantastic towers and spires, and countless prehistoric ruins and cave dwellings.

The Mormons, persecuted and expelled from a number of other states, began major settlements in Utah from 1847. From the time their leader Brigham Young said "This is the place," they have used irrigation farming to transform the agriculture of the state. Utah is a leading producer of copper, beryllium, gold, silver, lead, and uranium. Many minerals are extracted from the Great Salt Lake. Manufacturing, particularly of food products, steel, spacecraft, and electronic equipment, is increasing. Utah is also a popular tourist area.

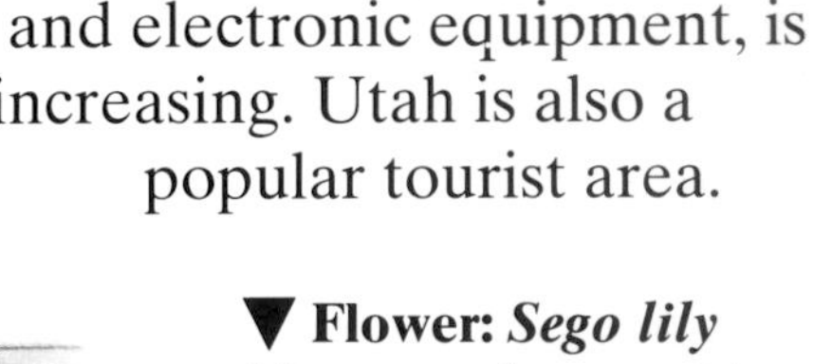

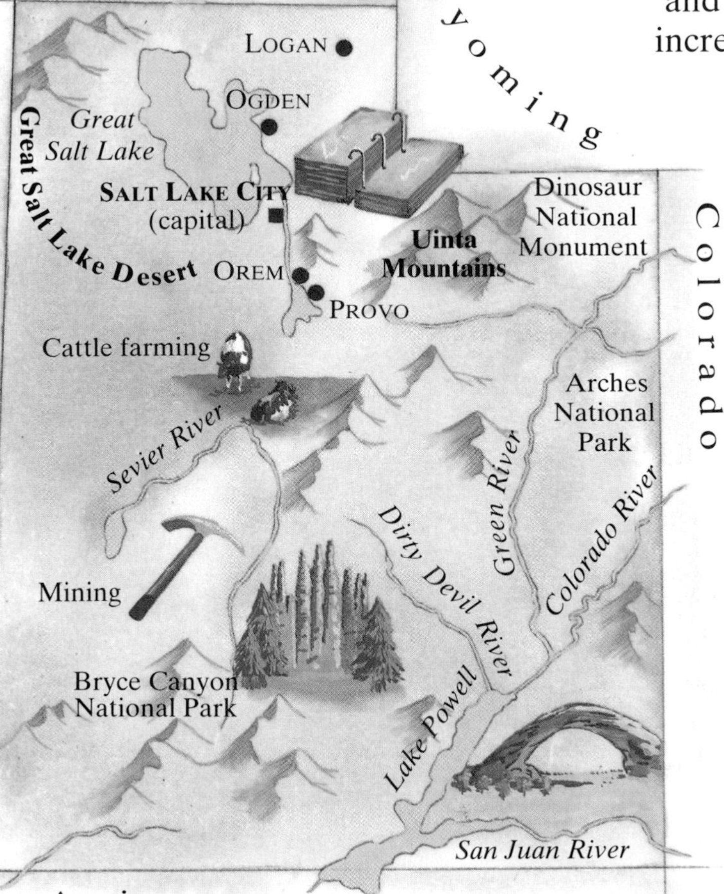

▼ State flag:
The two dates below the state coat of arms are 1847, when the Mormons settled in Utah, and 1896 when it joined the Union.

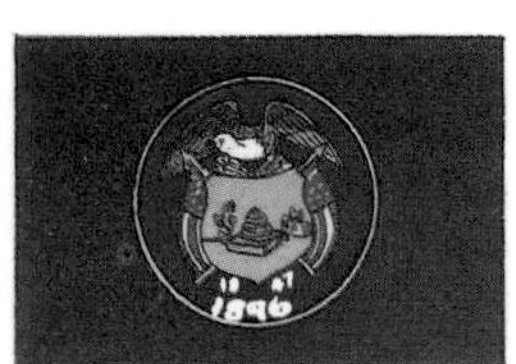

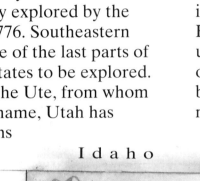

▼ Flower: ***Sego lily***
Most people grow this plant for its white flowers, but the bulb is edible.

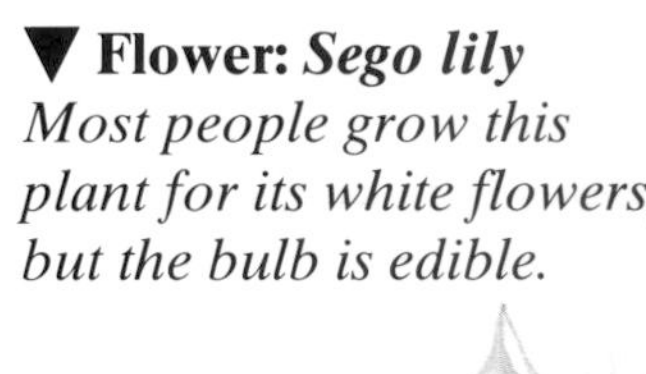

▼ Bird: ***Seagull***
This seabird is an unexpected state bird for a landlocked, largely desert state, but they are sometimes found near the lakes.

▶ Dinosaur National Monument
Dinosaur remains have been found in many parts of the state.

▶ Mormons
The Mormon headquarters are at Salt Lake City. Mormons base their faith on the Book of Mormon, which advocates self-help and a simple lifestyle, abstaining from alcohol and other stimulants.

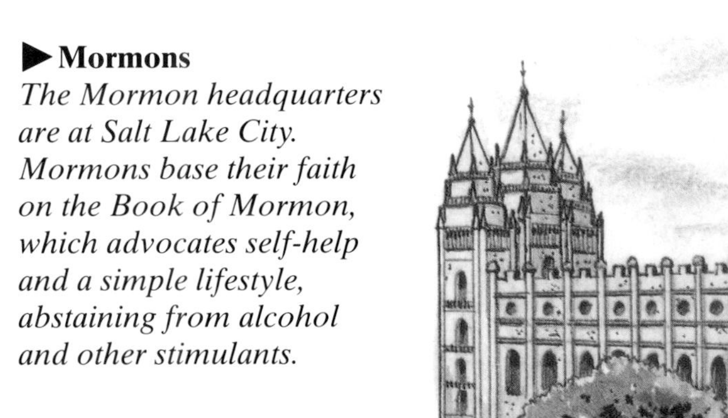

46

Oklahoma

The Sooner State

Motto:

Oklahoma joined the Union as the 46th state, on November 16 1907. Part of the Louisiana Purchase, it had previously been federally administered "Indian territory." White settlement began after the Civil War. The nickname "Sooner" comes from those settlers who left to claim land before the official start of the April 22 1889 land rush. Most of Oklahoma's Native Americans now live in the eastern part of the state, although the plains tribes have remained in the west.

Oklahoma has a diverse landscape with high uplands, vast windy plains, and rolling, wooded hills. Originally an agricultural state, farming was badly hit in the 1930s when drought caused much of the topsoil to blow away. Today, Oklahoma has a mixed economy. Most of its wealth comes from its raw materials including large deposits of oil, natural gas, and minerals. Cattle, wheat, and cotton are the main farm products. Local industries include food processing, oil refining, and engineering.

Kansas
Texas
Missouri
Ponca City
Wheat
Dairy and cattle farming
Tulsa
Lake Hudson
Cimarron River
Arkansas River
Oklahoma City (capital)
Canadian River
Arkansas
Wichita Mountains
Oil
Ouachita Mountains
Cotton
Lawton
Coal
Peanuts
Red River
Lake Texoma
Texas

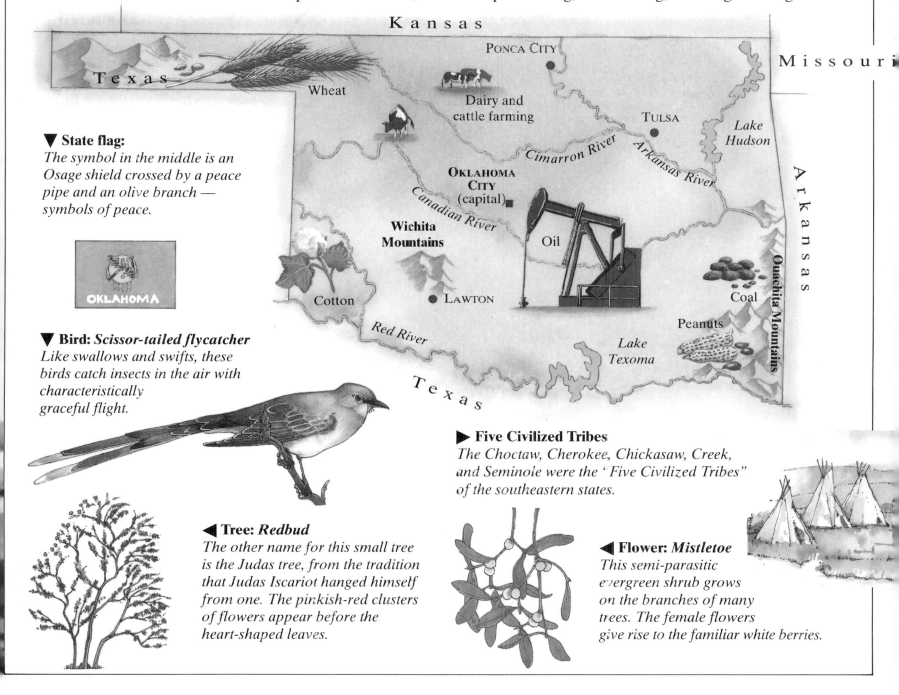

▼ State flag:
The symbol in the middle is an Osage shield crossed by a peace pipe and an olive branch — symbols of peace.

OKLAHOMA

▼ Bird: *Scissor-tailed flycatcher*
Like swallows and swifts, these birds catch insects in the air with characteristically graceful flight.

▶ Five Civilized Tribes
The Choctaw, Cherokee, Chickasaw, Creek, and Seminole were the "Five Civilized Tribes" of the southeastern states.

◀ Tree: *Redbud*
The other name for this small tree is the Judas tree, from the tradition that Judas Iscariot hanged himself from one. The pinkish-red clusters of flowers appear before the heart-shaped leaves.

◀ Flower: *Mistletoe*
This semi-parasitic evergreen shrub grows on the branches of many trees. The female flowers give rise to the familiar white berries.

47

New Mexico

The Land of Enchantment

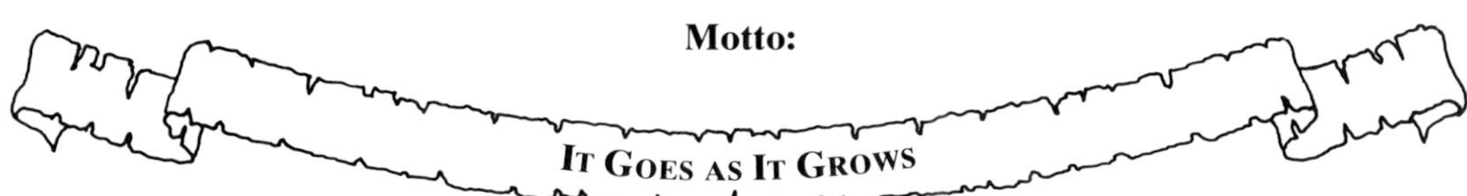

The 47th state to join the Union, New Mexico achieved statehood on January 6 1912. The name *Nuevo Mejico* dates back to at least 1582, about 50 years after the region was first explored by the Spanish.

Home to many tribes, including the Navajo and Apaches, the territory was taken from Mexico during the 1846–1848 war.

Traditionally rural, horses, mules, cattle, sheep, and hogs are raised in New Mexico. Grain, beans, and cotton are grown too. The state's copper mines are now much more important than the old gold, silver, lead, and zinc mines. There are also sand and gravel quarries, and cement works. New Mexico has many high-tech industries, including atomic research. A part of the "sun belt," thousands of tourists are attracted by the distinctive local culture and spectacular scenery. The incredible Carlsbad Caverns include a "room" some 1,200 feet long, 300 feet wide, and 300 feet high.

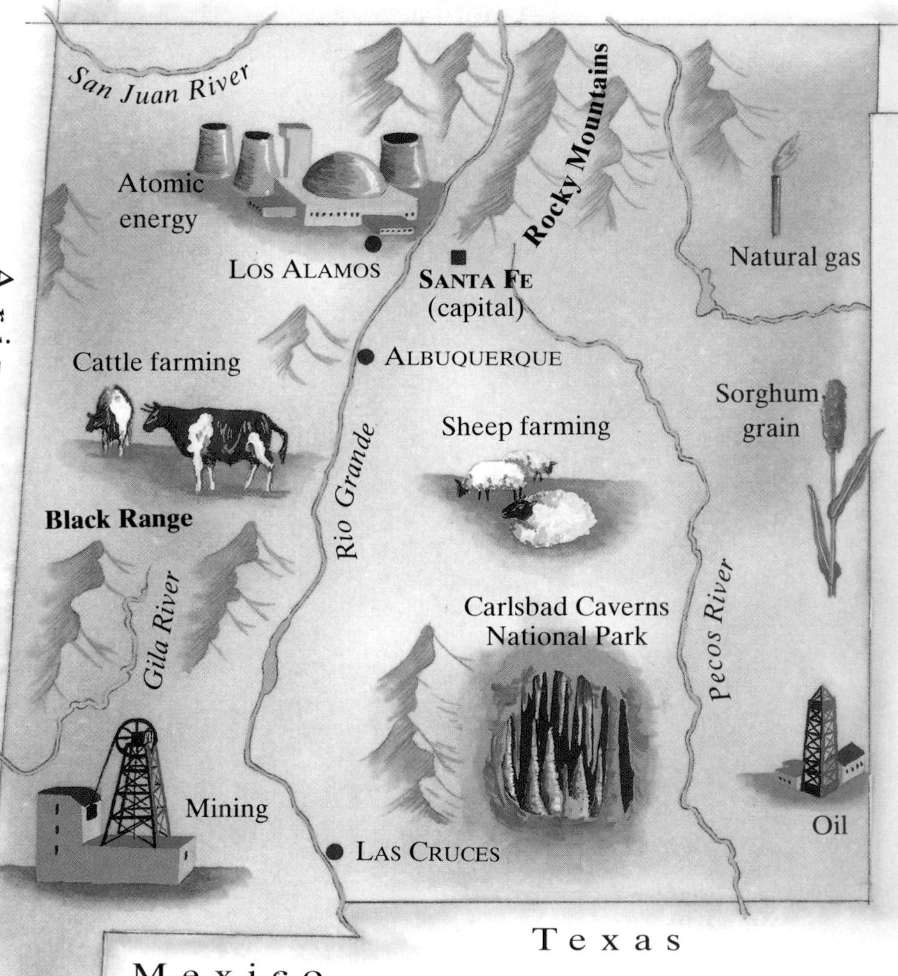

▶ **State flag:**
Red and yellow are the colors of Imperial Spain, and the center of the flag is an ancient Zuñi sun symbol.

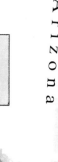

▶ **Tree: *Piñon***
The pine nuts from the piñon were a food source for the Zuñi Native Americans.

▼ **Bird: *Roadrunner***
This long-legged bird can run up to 15 miles per hour.

▶ **Flower: *Yucca***
This plant can reach over 12 feet high. A huge cone of flowers is borne above a crown of leaves.

▶ ***Adobe* buildings**
Adobe *or sun-dried brick was the usual building material in old New Mexico. It has left its stamp on the architecture of the state.*

Arizona

Grand Canyon State

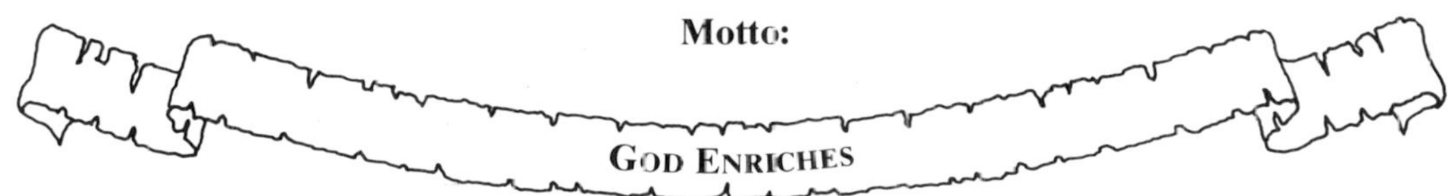

The arid lands of Arizona, the 48th state to join the Union, on February 14 1912, discouraged most of the early explorers. The area was ceded to the United States after the Mexican War. A classic symbol of America's "Old West," Arizona has a rich cultural heritage. Many Native American tribes were resettled in the area and there are still more Native Americans in Arizona than in any other state. The main tribes are the Navajo, Hopi, and Apache. They mostly live on reservations.

After the Civil War, two things encouraged white settlement: the discovery of gold and silver, and later of copper, and the success of irrigation for farming. Some rivers were diverted for irrigation, while others were dammed to produce hydroelectric power. Agriculture has continued to thrive, with cotton, grain, and livestock the leading produce. Industry and tourism have also contributed greatly to Arizona's prosperity.

◀ **The Grand Canyon**
A mile deep, an average of 10 miles wide, and about 220 miles long, the Grand Canyon is an amazing sight. The rocks at the bottom are two billion years old.

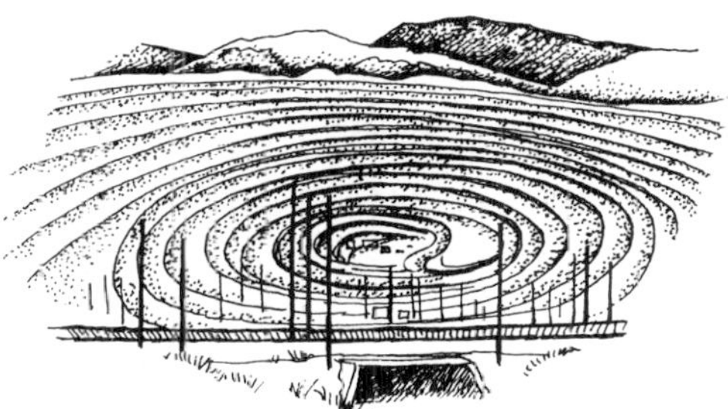

◀ **Mineral:** ***Copper***
Arizona's huge copper mines produce over half the nation's copper.

▲ **State flag:**
The colors of Spain (red and yellow) and of Arizona (blue and gold –sky and sand) are combined with a copper star.

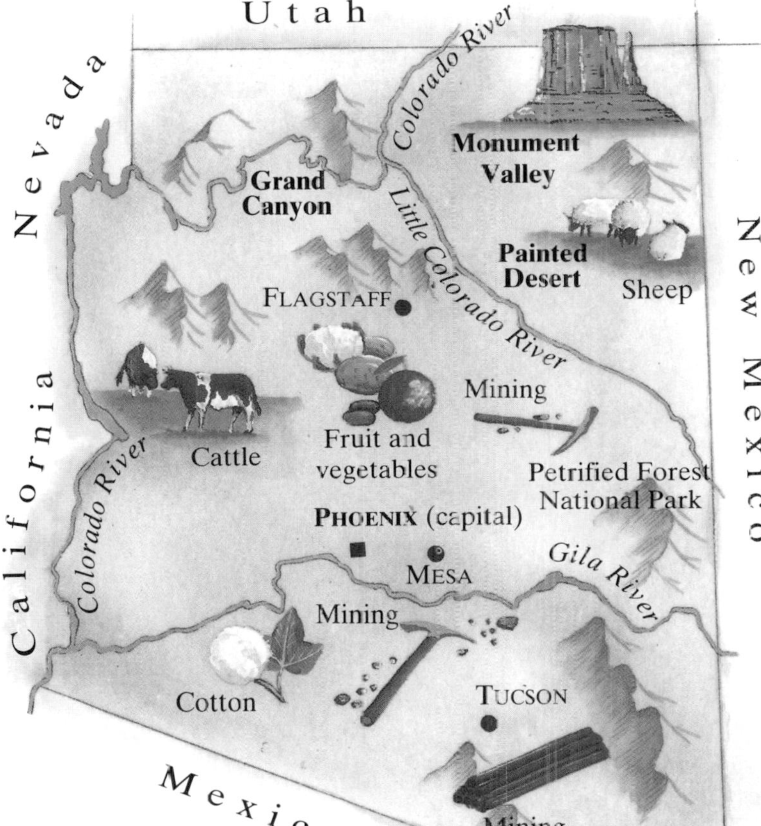

▲ **Petrified Forest National Park**
These ancient trees, millions of years old, have turned into multicolored stone.

▲ **Flower:** ***Saguaro cactus flower***
The saguaro cactus, a typical sight of the Arizona desert, can absorb and hold up to a ton of water.

▼ **Bird:** ***Cactus wren***
The cactus wren, the largest wren in North America, nests in the prickly cholla cactus.

Alaska

The Great Land

Motto:

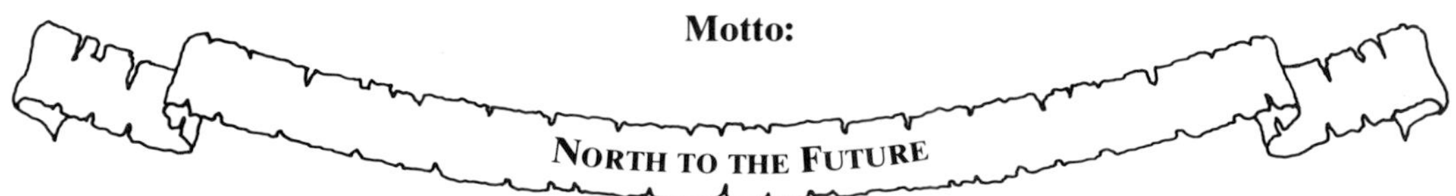

Alaska, then called Russian America, was bought from Russia in 1867 for $7,200,000. The Territory became the 49th state, on January 3 1959. Alaska is a huge, mountainous volcanic area almost twice as big as Texas — the next largest state. The Aleut, Inuit (formerly called Eskimo), and other Native Americans of the state were thinly spread, and there were not the forced migrations seen in other states. "Alaska" comes from the Aleut "al-ay-ek-sha," meaning "mainland."

For many years, immigration and settlement were very slow. The discovery of gold in the late 1800s led to a mining boom. Further explorations were undertaken and today the mineral wealth of Alaska — oil, metals, including uranium and platinum, natural gas, and coal — is the mainstay of its economy. Forestry, agriculture, and fishing are also important. Alaska's southern mountains and unspoilt wilderness are a growing tourist attraction. There are few major roads, so light aircraft are the main form of transport for long trips, while snowmobiles are used in the frozen North.

▶ **State flag:**
The flag, designed by a 13-year-old schoolboy, shows eight gold stars — the Big Dipper and Polaris.

▶ **Mineral: *Gold***
The Klondike in 1896 was only one of many "gold rushes" sparked by the discovery of gold from 1880 onwards.

▲ **Fish: *King salmon***
The cold-water game fish of Alaska are among the biggest and strongest in the world.

▼ **Sport: *Dog mushing***
Sleds drawn by Husky dogs were used as a way of shifting heavy loads before snowmobiles were invented.

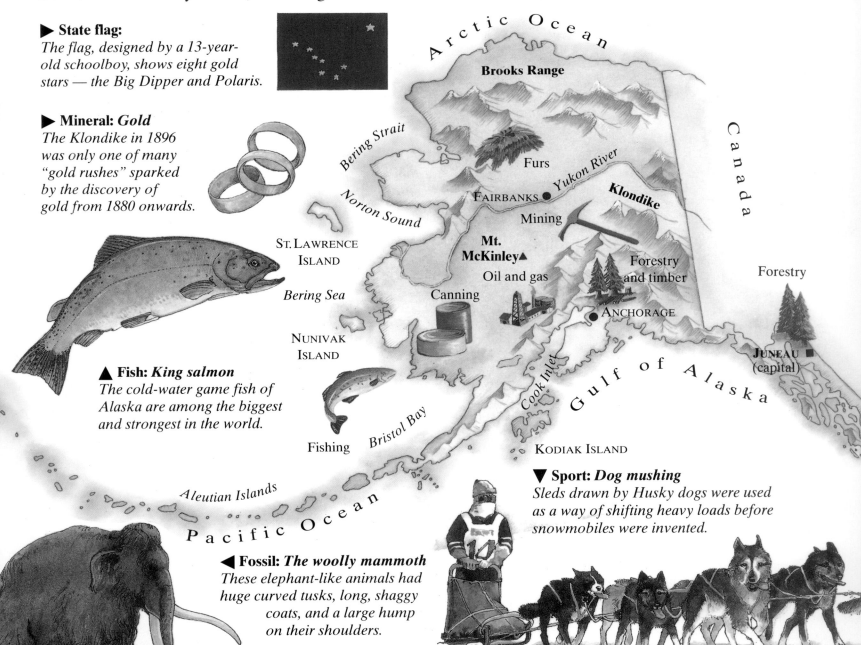

◀ **Fossil: *The woolly mammoth***
These elephant-like animals had huge curved tusks, long, shaggy coats, and a large hump on their shoulders.

Hawaii

The Aloha State

Motto:

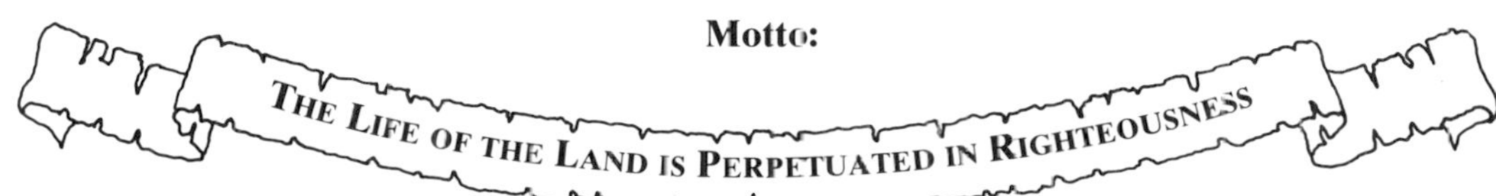

Hawaii, a part of what was once called the Sandwich Islands, was the 50th state to join the Union, on August 21 1959. Almost 2,400 miles from the American mainland, Hawaii was probably settled by Polynesians about a thousand years ago. The islands are now home to an incredibly diverse mix of people: aside from the Polynesians, people of European, Japanese, Filipino, Korean, and African heritage have settled here.

Hawaii was first discovered by Captain Cook in 1778. The islands remained independent until they were annexed by the United States in 1898 at the request of the Hawaiian people. The bravery of Hawaiians in World War II is widely believed to have led to Hawaii being granted statehood.

The lush tropical vegetation, beautiful beaches, and soaring volcanic mountains attract thousands of visitors each year, making tourism Hawaii's largest industry. Conservation measures have been taken to prevent over-development. Agriculture is subtropical, and Hawaii is noted for pineapples, sugar cane, orchids, and other flowers.

▶ **Tree:** ***Kukui (Candlenut)***
This useful tree can be used to make oil, dyes, paint, gum, food, and medicine, as well as candles.

◀ **Flower:**
Yellow hibiscus
This tropical plant has large sweet-smelling golden flowers.

KAUAI
Sugarcane
LIHUE
NIIHAU
Kualakahi Channel
Kauai Channel

▲ **State flag:**
No one knows why the British flag is present, but it was incorporated in an earlier version at least as far back as 1816.

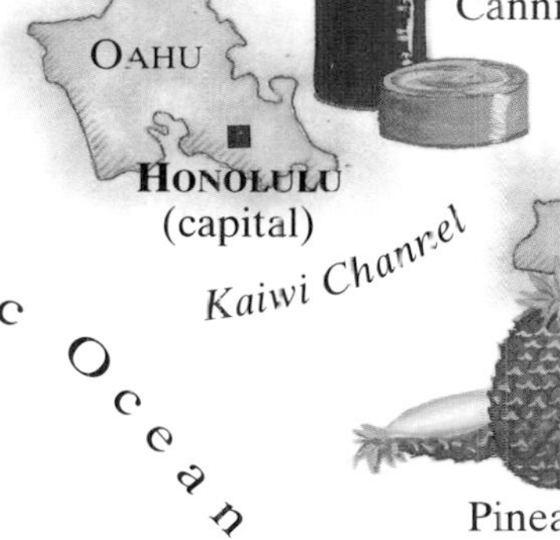

Pacific Ocean
Kaiwi Channel

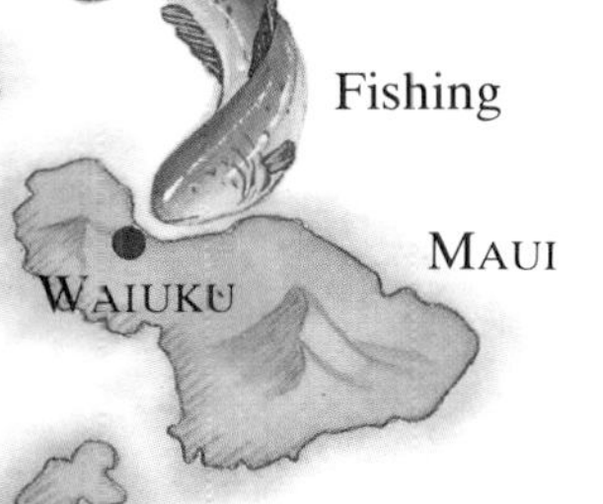

Alenuihaha Channel
Pacific Ocean

▶ **Surfing**
Surfing seems to have been a Hawaiian, or at least Polynesian, invention and Hawaii is the world mecca for surfers.

◀ **Bird:** ***Nene***
The big Hawaiian wild goose is now a rare protected species.

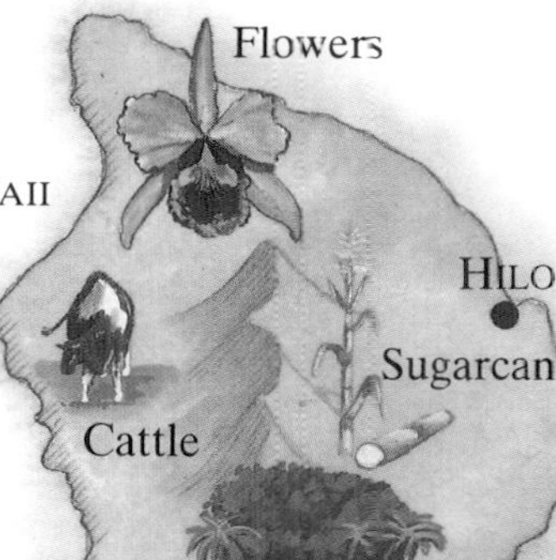

Index